HOMO SAPIENS ALPHABET

HOW TO GROW YOUR CLIENT BASE AND ENLIST THEM AS YOUR RAVING FANS BY THOROUGHLY UNDERSTANDING THEIR PHYSICAL TRAITS AND INHERENT BEHAVIORS.

BY

ANHVIET NGUYEN

THIS BOOK IS DEDICATED TO MY MOM, QUY TRUONG,

WHO HAS UNDERSTOOD AND SUPPORTED MY CRAZINESS IN TRYING TO FIND MY TRUE CALLING, TRAVELING, AND WHO HAS COOLLY WITHSTOOD BARRAGES OF INQUIRES AND CRITICISM FROM RELATIVES ABOUT MY CRAZINESS. SHE IS THE TOUGHEST AND THE MOST GENEROUS WOMAN I KNOW.

ISBN: 1468143778
ISBN-13: 978-1468143775
First Edition

TABLE OF CONTENT

INTRODUCTION

INTRODUCTION

WHY YOU SHOULD READ THIS BOOK.

I am writing this book to share with you the benefits of understanding your fellow men's unchanged physical traits and their innate behaviors. Sale is all about providing the products and services that your clients want and need. Knowing their natural tendencies will help you anticipate and serve their needs and wants the best you can. Also, knowing their preferred method of collaboration ameliorates your communication with them and helps you foster a harmonious relationship with your clients and thus cultivate lifetime clients and an army of raving fans.

I have been working in sales and marketing for more than 10 years. Before that, I was a lab rat working in Research and Development Lab at Biotechnology and Pharmaceutical companies. I was unhappy in that line of work; so I wanted to look for other career. Through sheer luck, I had an epiphany that in order to be successful in life, I needed to learn how to sell. Everything we do, we have to sell. For example, a dentist has to sell his service to his patients (clients) if he wants them as repeat patients. A lawyer has to sell his service to his clients if he wants them to keep using his legal services.

Acting on this epiphany, I decided to go back to school to learn. I enrolled in the MBA program to learn about business. In retrospect, it may not have been the best course of action. It didn't teach me much about sales, but it sure got me into a mountain of debt, on top of an existing sizable mountain. So, I decided to take some time off to backpack through Southeast Asia. I managed to convince a couple friends to quit their well-paid jobs to travel with me. Many months later, when I came back to the States, I jumped into real estate sales to learn how to sell. If I could earn the trust of people who invest a large sum into a house, I would be successful at helping people obtaining what they need and want. I was struggling and fumbling along. A sale is mostly commission based. No sales, No money. I had to start making money. So, I read books, attended seminars, picked the brain of the other successful salesmen, and anything I could think of to help improve my sales skill. I have learned some pretty good sales systems like By Referral Only, or techniques in reading body language, etc. I have used these systems and have had some success. Regardless of what you sell such as a house, an airplane, a refrigerator, a car, or a service, you have to sell it to a person or persons. It all comes down to the personal selling. It is the human relationship that wins you that sales contract. It is the mutual trust you must garner.

In selling real estate, it is a service promised to be rendered. Clients don't know how good it is until the transaction ends. Anyone can claim to be the best, to be number one. How do clients choose a real estate agent when they need one? It is considered to be one of the biggest investments of one's life. What I have learned is that they choose me because they like me as a person and feel that I am trustworthy and I will serve their needs and wants to the best of my ability. I would genuinely have to try to do the best I could to serve their needs and wants. When everything is done, we will know if the service is up to their expectations or not.

Assuming that you are a capable professional, singing up clients is a matter of whether or not they like and trust you. If you can understand their needs, wants, and how they prefer to conduct business reasonably well and communicate with them how you plan on working with them and helping them meet these needs and wants, they will be your clients for life. Every good salesman has tried to learn how to read and understand the other fellows and has become masterful at it. Some are born with some basic people skills that can be polished to be a great salesman. Mike V, a fellow real estate agent, is a good example of a salesman with keen understanding of his clients' needs and wants. Most of us have to learn through trials and errors; but it is definitely learnable. Through my years of selling, travelling, continuous learning, researching, I have accumulated a simple process to identify people's physical traits and to understand their correlated innate behaviors. The study of physical traits has been around for thousands of years in China. I have attempted to learn the Chinese way of reading physical traits but I was unsuccessful because it is too complicated. This subject is also studied and applied in the United States by Elsie Benedicts more than 100 years ago. She illustrated this seemingly complicated subject in a simple, easy to understand context. Mastering this knowledge will help you win more devoted clients, enlist them as your sneezers, and ultimately increase your sales and income tremendously.

Many fortune tellers I met have told me that I am a creative person and should work within that field, that I am smart, that I will be wealthy, and that I work well with people… Now I understand that they had gleaned all these things from my physical traits. I am predominantly a Flushed type with a secondary Brainy physical trait. As you read the chapters in this book, you will also understand why. I recommend that you should read each type carefully while thinking of your friend, family members, co-workers, or boss whom you know well and who belongs predominantly to this type. Take the behaviors I provide for each type and compare them with what you know about them. You will be surprised of how accurate you are. You know yourself best. So, when you read, try to identify which type you are mainly and how your behaviors can be explained according to your physical traits.

Let's get started.

THE HOMO SAPIENS ALPHABET

> *Fundamental traits of every individual are indelibly stamped in the shape of his body, head, face and hands, and even in his walk and voice—understanding this alphabet, you can read the characteristics of any person on sight.*

Significance of Size, Shape and Structure

All dogs belong to the same species but there is a great difference between the "nature" of a St. Bernard and that of a Terrier, just as there is a decided difference between the natures of different human beings. But in both instances the actions, reactions and habits of each can be accurately anticipated on sight by the shape, size and structure of the two creatures.

Correlation of Body and Brain

Man, a highly evolved creature, who not only acts, but thinks and feels. All these thoughts, feelings and emotions are strongly correlated. The body and the mind of man are so closely bound together that whatever affects one affects the other. An instantaneous change of mind instantly changes the muscles of the face. A violent thought instantly brings violent bodily movements like clenching of a fist, tightening of the jaw...

Homo sapiens Alphabet

Tells Fundamentals

How much do external characteristics tell about a man? They tell, with amazing accuracy, all the basic, fundamental principal traits of his nature. The size, shape and structure of a man's body tell more important facts about his real self, what he thinks and what he does.

Reading People

Learning to read men and women is a more delightful process than learning to read books. Every person you see is a true story, more romantic and absorbing than anything bound in covers. Learning to read people is also a simpler process than learning to read books because there are fewer letters in the human alphabet. To the untrained eye, man seems like a mystifying crossword puzzle. Understanding the rules and patterns, you will know how to read him; he is not difficult to analyze.

Only a Few Feelings

This is because there are after all but a few kinds of human feelings. Some form of hunger, love, hate, fear, hope or ambition gives rise to every human emotion and every human thought.

Thoughts Bring Actions

Now our actions follow our thoughts. Every thought, however transitory, causes muscular action, which leaves its trace in that part of the physical organism which is most closely allied to it.

Physiology and Psychology Interwoven

Homo sapiens Alphabet

Look into the mirror the next time you are angry, happy, surprised, tired, or sorrowful and note the changes caused by your emotions in your facial muscles. Constant repetition of the same kinds of thoughts or emotions finally makes permanent changes in that part of the body which is physiologically related to these mental processes.

Law of Size

The larger any part or organ the better its equipment for carrying out the work of that organ and the more does it tend to express itself. Nature IS an efficiency expert and doesn't give you an oversupply of anything without demanding that you use it.

Survival of the Fittest

Nature has no accidents, she wastes no material and everything has a purpose. If you put up a good fight to live she will usually come to your rescue and give you enough of whatever is needed to tide you over. If you don't, she says you are not fit to occupy the earth and lets you go without grief. Thus she weeds out all but the strong—and evolution marches on.

Causes of Racial Characteristics

This inherent potentiality for altering the organism to meet the demands of the environment is especially noticeable in races and is the reason for most racial differences.

Differences in environment—climate, altitude and topography necessitated most of these physical differentiations which today enable us to know at a glance whether a man belongs to the European race, the Asian race, or the African race. The results of these differentiations and modifications will be told in the various chapters of this book.

Types Earlier than Races

The student of Human Analysis reads the disposition and nature of every individual with ease regardless of whether that individual be an American, a Frenchman, or a Chinese, because Human Analysis explains those fundamental traits which run through every race, color and nationality, according to the externals which always go with those traits.

Five Biological Types

Human Analysis differs from every other system of character analysis in that it classifies man into five types according to his biological evolution.

It deals with man in the light of the scientific discoveries. It estimates each individual according to his physical qualities. In other words, it looks at his externals and determines what Mother Nature has bestowed upon him to help him survive and thrive in this world.

Do What We Want to Do

It is easy to know what an individual will do under most circumstances because every human being does what he *wants* to do in the *way* he prefers to do it *most* of the time. If you doubt it try this test: bring to mind any intimate friends, or even that of a husband or wife, and note how few changes they have made in their way of doing things in twenty years!

Homo sapiens Alphabet

Inborn Preferences

Every human being is born with preferences which manifest themselves from earliest childhood to death. These inborn tendencies are never obliterated and seldom controlled to any great extent, and then only by few individuals who have learned the power of the mind over the body. Besides a few who can learn this skill, most of the people on earth are blindly following the dictates of their inborn propensities.

The Hold of Habit

Look around you in shopping malls, office, or home and you will find that the quick, alert, impulsive man is acting quickly, alertly and impulsively most of the time. Nothing less than a calamity slows him down and then only temporarily; while the slow, patient, mild and passive individual is acting slowly, patiently, mildly and passively in spite of all provocations. Some overwhelming passion or crisis may speed him up momentarily but as soon as it fades he reverts to his old slow habits.

Significance of Flesh, Bone and Muscle

Human Analysis is the science which shows you how to recognize the slow man, the quick man, the stubborn man, the yielding man, the leader, the learner, and all other basic kinds of men on sight from the shape, size and structure of their bodies.

Certain body shapes indicate predispositions to fleshiness, leanness, boniness, muscularity and braininess, and this predisposition is so much ingrained in the individual that he cannot disguise it. The urge given him by this inborn mechanism is so strong as to be practically irresistible. Every experience of his life calls forth some kind of reaction and invariably the reaction will be similar, in every fundamental characteristic, to the reactions of other people who have bodies of the same general size, shape and structure as his own.

Succeed at What We Like

No person achieves success or happiness when compelled to do what he naturally dislikes to do. Since these likes and dislikes stay with him to the grave, one of the biggest modern problems is that of helping men and women to discover and to capitalize their inborn traits.

Enthusiasm and Self-Expression

Every individual does best those things which permit him to act in accordance with his natural inclinations. This explains why we like best those things we do best. It takes real enthusiasm to make a success of any undertaking, for nothing less than enthusiasm can turn on a full gush.

We struggle from the cradle to the grave for self-expression. Everything that pushes us in a direction opposed to our natural tendencies is done half-heartedly, inefficiently and disgruntledly. These are the steps that lead straight to failure. Failure can be avoided and success can be achieved by every normal person if he understands his natural calling and follows it.

Five Makes of Human Cars

There are five makes or types of human cars, differing as definitely in size, shape and structure as Volvo differ from Ferrari. Each human type differs as widely in its capacities, possibilities and aptitudes as a Volvo differs from a Ferrari. Like the Volvo or Ferrari, the externals indicate these functional differences with unfailing accuracy. Furthermore just as a Volvo never changes into a Ferrari or a Ferrari into a Volvo, a human being never changes his type. He may modify it, polish it, or add a powerful engine to it; but it will never change.

Cannot be Deceived.

The student of Human Analysis cannot be deceived as to the type of any individual any more than you can be deceived about the make of a car.

One may "doll up" a Volvo to his heart's content—remove the hood and top and put on custom-made substitutes—it is still a Volvo, always will be a Volvo and you can always detect that it is a Volvo. It will do valuable, necessary things but only those things it was designed to do and in its own particular manner; neither could a Ferrari act like a Volvo.

Are You a Volvo or a Ferrari?

So it is with human cars. Maybe you have been awed by the jewels and clothes with which many human Volvo disguise themselves. The chances are that you have overlooked a dozen Ferrari this week because their paint was rusty. Perhaps you are a Ferrari yourself, drawing a Volvo salary because you don't know you are a high-powered machine capable of making ten times the speed you have been making on your highway of life.

Superficialities Sway Us

If so, your mistake is only natural. The world classifies human beings according to their veneer. To the world, a human motorcycle can pass for a Rolls-Royce any day if sufficiently camouflaged with diamonds, expensive fashion, exclusive club membership, and expensive house, etc…

Don't Judge by the Cover

Nothing is more unsafe than to attempt to judge the actual natures of people by their clothes, houses, religious faith, political affiliations, prejudices, dialect, etiquette or customs. These are only the veneer laid on by upbringing, teachers, preachers, traditions and other forces of suggestion, and it is a veneer so thin that takes very little to scratch it off.

The Truth Always There

But the real individual is always there, filled with the tendencies of his type, bending always toward them, constantly seeking opportunities to run as he was built to run; forever striving toward self-expression. It is this ever-active urge which causes him to revert, in the manifold activities of everyday life, to the methods, manners and peculiarities common to his type.

This means that unless he gets into an environment, a vocation and a marriage which permits him to do what he *wants* to do he will be miserable, inefficient, unsuccessful and sometimes criminal.

It is as vain to expect to eradicate these inborn trends and put others in their places as to make a sewing machine out of an airplane or an oak out of a pine. The most man can do for his fellowman is to understand and inspire him. The most he can do for himself is to understand and organize his inborn capacities.

These Rules Are Your Tools

These rules are scientific. They are true and they are true always. They are very valuable tools for the continuance of your progress through life.

An understanding of people is the greatest weapon you can possess. Therefore these are the most precious tools you can own. But like every tool in the world and all knowledge in the world, they must be used as they were built to be used or you will get little service out of them.

You would not expect to run a car properly without paying the closest attention to the rules for clutches, brakes, starters and gears. Everything scientific is based not on guesses but laws. The techniques of analyzing people by physical traits are as scientific as the automobile. It will carry you far and do it easily if you will do your part. Your part consists of learning the few simple rules laid down in this book and in applying them in the everyday affairs of your life.

IMPORTANT

The Five Extremes

Homo sapiens Alphabet

This book deals with PURE or UNMIXED types only. When you understand these, the significance of their several combinations as seen in everyday life will be clear to you.

Founded in Five Biological Systems

Each PURE type is the result of the over-development of one of the five biological systems possessed by all human beings—the digestive, circulatory, muscular, skeletal, or brain.

Therefore every individual exhibits to some degree the characteristics of all the five types.

Combinations Common in America

The average American man or woman is a COMBINATION of some two of these types with a third discernible in the background.

To Analyze People

To understand human beings familiarize yourself first with the PURE or UNMIXED types and then it will be easy and fascinating to spell out their combinations and what they mean in the people all about you.

Postpone Combinations

Until you have learned these pure types thoroughly, it will be to your advantage to forget that there is such a thing as combinations. After you have these extreme types well in mind you will be ready to analyze combinations.

Homo sapiens Alphabet

The Five Types

Science has discovered that there are five types of human beings. Discarding for a moment their technical names, they may be called the Fleshy people, the Flushed people, the Muscular people, the Bony people, and the Brainy people.

Each varies from the others in shape, size and structure and is recognizable at a glance by his physique or build. This is because his type is determined by the predominance within his body of one of the five great departments or biological systems—the digestive, the circulatory, the muscular, the skeletal or the nervous.

At Birth

Every child is born with one of these systems more highly developed, larger and better equipped than the others.

Type Never Disappears

Throughout his life this system will express itself more, be more intense and constant in its functioning than the others. Training, education, environment or experience can alter some minor behaviors. However, as long he is in normal health, the predominance of this system doesn't change. His type still dictates his likes, dislikes and most of his reactions.

I would recommend that you read and study each type until you thoroughly internalize it before you go to the next type.

Good journey!

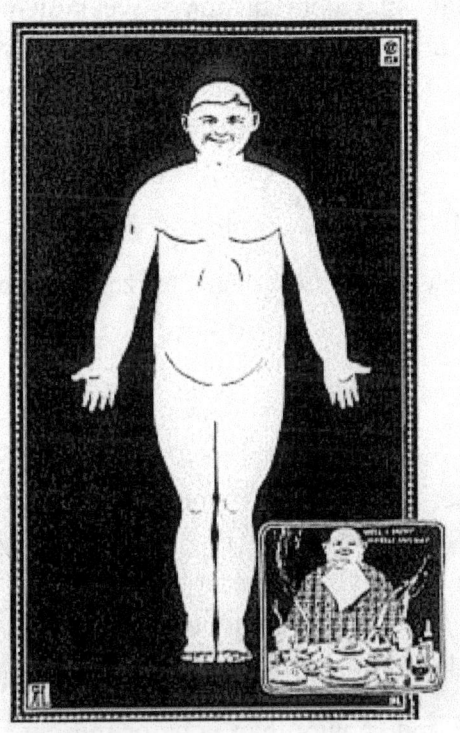

CHAPTER I

THE FLESHY TYPE

"The Enjoyer"

Shawn, a roommate of mine at UC Davis, belongs to this body type. He had all the characteristics of this type. Whenever he was not in class, he usually was eating something. He was fleshy but always jolly. In his room, there was a big Lazy Boy armchair where he sits to watch TV and to play Nintendo games. Most people liked him. He got along with almost everyone and he avoided confrontation at all cost.

Those individuals in whom the digestive system is more highly developed than any other are called the Fleshy type. The digestive system consists of the stomach, small and large intestines, esophagus and every part of the digestive apparatus.

Physical Roundness

A general roundness of outline characterizes this type. He is round in every direction.

The Overweight Individual

Soft flesh thickly padded over a small-boned body distinguishes the pure Fleshy type. In men of this type the largest part of the body is around the girth, in women it is around the hips. These always indicate a large digestive system in good working order. Fat is the surplus tissue—the amount manufactured by the digestive system over and above the needs of the body.

Fat is more soft and spongy than bone or muscle and thus lends its wearer a softer structure and appearance.

Small Hands and Feet

Because his bones are small, the pure Fleshy has small feet and small hands. How many times you have noted with surprise that the two hundred pound person had tiny feet! The inconvenience of "getting around" which you have noticed in her is due to the fact that while she has more weight to carry, she has smaller than average feet with which to do it with.

The Pure Fleshy Head

Homo sapiens Alphabet

A head that is comparatively small for the body is another characteristic of the extreme Fleshy. The neck and lower part of the head are covered with rolls of blubber. This gives the head the effect of spreading outward from the crown as it goes down to the neck, thus giving the neck a short, disproportionately large appearance.

The Fleshy-Faced Person

A "full-moon" face with double or triple chins gives this man his "baby face." Look carefully at any extremely round person and you will see that his features are inclined to the same immaturity of form that characterizes his body.

Very few round men have long noses. Nearly all round men and women have not only shorter, rounder noses but shorter upper lips, fuller mouths, rounder eyes and more youthful expressions than other people—in short, the features of childhood.

The entire physical makeup of this type is modeled upon the circle— round hands with dimples where the knuckles are supposed to be; round fingers, round waist, round limbs, sloping shoulders, curving thighs, bulging calves, wrists and ankles.

Wherever you see curves predominating in the physical outlines of any person, that person is largely of the Fleshy type and will exhibit the Fleshy traits.

The Man of Few Movements

The Fleshy man is a man of unhurried, undulating movements. The difficulty in moving large bodies quickly necessitates a slowing down of all his activities. These people are easeful in their actions, make as few moves as possible and thereby lend an air of restfulness wherever they go.

 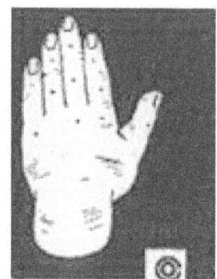

Typical Facial Features and Hand of the Fleshy Type

The Fleshy Man's Walk

Abundantly fleshy people waddle when they walk, though few of them realize it.

Spilling Over Chairs

The round man spills over chairs and out of his clothes. Big arm chairs, big cushy sofas, and spacious cars are a must for these men. Note the bee-line the round person makes for the big leather chair when he enters a room!

Clothes for Comfort

The best that money can buy are the kinds of clothes purchased by the Fleshy whenever he can afford them. And it often happens that he can afford them, especially if the Brainy system comes second in his makeup. If he is in middle circumstances his clothes will be chosen chiefly for comfort. Even the rich Fleshy "gets into something loose" as soon as he is alone. Baggy clothes are seen most frequently on them.

Comfort is one of the very first aims of this type. To attain it he often wears old shoes or gloves long past their time to save breaking in a new pair.

How the Fleshy Man Talks

Never to take anything too seriously is an unconscious policy of round people. They show it plainly in their actions and speech. The very round man is seldom a brilliant conversationalist. He is often a "jollier" and tells stories well, especially anecdotes and personal experiences.

Doesn't Tell His Troubles

He seldom relates his troubles and often appears not to have any. He avoids references to *-isms and -ology* and eschews all who discuss them. Radical groups seldom number any extremely round men among their members, and when they do it is usually for some other purpose than those mentioned in the by-laws.

The very round man dislikes argument, avoids disagreeing directly with you, and sticks to the outer edges of serious questions in his social conversation.

The round Man "Lives to Eat"

Rich food in large quantities is enjoyed by the average round man three times a day and three hundred and sixty-five days a year. Between meals he usually manages to stow away a generous supply of junk foods. They kept junk food companies in business.

The Deep Mystery

"What do you suppose is making me so plump?" naively inquires the round man when it finally occurs to him—as it did to his friends long before—that he is surely and speedily taking on flesh.

If you don't know the answer, look at the table of any fleshy person in any restaurant, café or all-you-can-eat restaurant. He is eating with as much enthusiasm as if he had just been rescued from a forty-day fast. He looked an equally generous meal in the eye and put it all in his belly.

Fleshy-Making Foods

Foods rich in fat and carbohydrate increase your weight just as fast as you eat them, if your digestive system is anything like it should be. Though he is the last man in the world who ought to indulge in them, the fleshy man likes these foods above all others. When compelled to have a meal without them, he feels as though he hadn't eaten at all.

An Experiment

Go to a buffet type restaurant and watch what Fleshy people choose to eat. Without exception their trays came by heaped with fatty foods, high carbohydrate foods, and high protein food.

Digestion and Contentment

The eating of delicious food is one of the most intense and poignant pleasures of life. The digestion of food, when one possesses the splendid machinery for it which characterizes the Fleshy, gives a deep feeling of serenity and contentment. Since the Fleshy man is always just going to a big meal or in the process of digesting one he does not give himself a chance to become ill natured. His own and the world's troubles sit lightly upon him.

Likes Complacent People

People who take things as they find them are the ones the Fleshy prefers for friends, not only because, like the rest of us, he likes his own kind of folks, but because the other kind seem incongruous to him. He takes the attitude that resistance is a waste of energy. He knows other and easier ways of getting what he desires.

There are types who take a lively interest in those who are different from them, but not the Fleshy. He prefers easy-going, hospitable, complacent friends whose homes and hearts are always open and whose minds run on the simple, personal things.

The reason for this is obvious. All of us like the people, situations, experiences and environments which bring out our natural tendencies, which call into play those reflexes and reactions to which we tend naturally.

Chooses Food-Loving Friends

"Let's have something to eat" is a phrase whose hospitality has broken more ice and warmed more hearts than any other, unless perchance that rapidly disappearing "let's have something to drink."

Homo sapiens Alphabet

The Fleshy person keeps at the top of his list those homey souls who set a good table and excel in the art of third and fourth helpings.

Because he is a very adaptable sort of individual, this type can reconcile himself to the other kind whenever it serves his purpose. But the tender spots in his heart are reserved for those who encourage him in his favorite indoor sport.

When He Doesn't Like You

A Fleshy man seldom dislikes anybody very hard or for very long. Really disliking anybody requires the expenditure of a good deal of energy and hating people is the most strenuous work in the world. So the Fleshy refuses to take even his dislikes to heart. He is a consistent energy saver and this fact is one of the secrets of his success. He applies this principle to everything in life. So he travels smoothly through his dealings with others.

Holds Few Grudges

"Forget it" is another phrase originated by the Fleshy people. You will hear them say it more often than any other type. And what is more, they excel the rest of us in putting it into practice. The result is that their nerves are usually in better working order. This type runs down his batteries less frequently than any other.

Avoids the "-Ologists"

When he takes the trouble to think about it there are a few kinds of people the Fleshy does not care for. The man who is bent on discussing the problems of the universe, the highbrow who wants to practice his new relativity lecture on him, the theorist who is given to lengthy description, and all advocates of new -isms and -ology are avoided by the pure Fleshy. He calls them obsessives, fanatics and fools.

When he sees a highbrow approaching, instead of having it out with him as some of the other types would, he finds he has important business somewhere else. Thus he preserves his temperature, something that in the average fleshy man seldom goes far above normal.

Describes His Food

The Fleshy person likes to regale you with alluring descriptions of what he had for breakfast, what he has ordered for lunch and what he is planning for dinner—and the tidbits he has on the program for after the theater.

How Each Finds Happiness

We live for happiness and each type finds its greatest happiness in following those innate urges determined by the most highly-developed system in its makeup. The Fleshy man's disposition, nature, character and personality are built by and around his digestive system. He is happiest when gratifying it and whenever he shuns it he is miserable, just as the rest of us are when we ignore our predominant system.

Enjoyment the Keynote of This Type

The good things of life—rich, abundant food and everything that serves the personal appetites—are the cravings of this type. He purchases and uses more of the limousines, chefs, and comfort goods than any other three types combined, and gets more for his money out of them than others do. The keynote of his nature is personal enjoyment. His senses of touch and taste are also especially acute.

The Fleshy Man Loves Comfort

You can tell a great deal about a man's type by noting for what classes of things he spends most of his extra money. The Fleshy may have no insurance, no savings, or no real estate but he will have all the modern comforts he can possibly afford.

Many of the world's millionaires belong to the Fleshy type and Human Analysis explains why. We make few efforts in life except to satisfy our most urgent demands, desires, and ambitions. Each human type differs in its cravings from each of the others and takes the respective means necessary to gratify these cravings. The Fleshy craves those luxuries, comforts and conveniences which only money can procure for him.

The Fleshy Millionaire

When the Fleshy is a man of brains, he uses his brains to get money. No Fleshy person enjoys work but the greater his brain capacity is, the more will he forego leisure to make money to supply him the comfort.

When the Fleshy Man is in Average Circumstances

Any man's money-making ambitions depend largely on whether money is essential to the satisfaction of his predominating instincts. If he is Fleshy and of average brain capacity, he will overcome his physical more than enough to secure for him and his family most of the comforts of modern life. The average-brained Fleshy man composes a large percentage of our population and the above accounts for his deserved reputation as a generous husband and father.

The Fleshy Man, a Good Provider

The Fleshy man will give his last cent to his wife and children for the things they desire but he is not inclined as much as some other types to listen to the miseries of the world at large. The Fleshy man is essentially a family man, a home man, a respectable, home-owning, tax-paying, peace-loving citizen.

Not a Reformer

He inclines to the belief that other families, other communities, other classes and other countries should work out their own salvation and he leaves them to do it. In all charitable, philanthropic and community "drives" he gives freely but is not lavished or sentimental about it. It is often a "business proposition" with him.

When the Fleshy Man is Poor

Love of ease is the Fleshy man's worst enemy. His inherent contentment accentuated by the inconvenience of moving about easily or quickly, constantly tempts him to let things slide. When he lacks the brain capacity for figuring out ways and means for getting things easily he is seldom a success at anything.

When the extreme Fleshy man's mentality is below the average he often refuses to work—in which case he becomes a familiar figure around parks and homeless shelters. Such a man finally graduates into the class of professional chair-warmers.

Fleshy People Love Leisure

Homo sapiens Alphabet

A chance to do as we please, especially to do as little hard work as possible, is a secret desire of almost everybody. But the Fleshy man takes the prize for wanting it most.

Not a Strenuous Worker

He is not constructed to work hard like some of the other types, as we shall see in subsequent chapters. His overweight is not only a handicap in that it slows down his movements, but it tends to slow down all his vital processes as well and to overload his heart. This gives him a chronic feeling of heaviness and inertia.

Everybody Likes Him

But Mother Nature must have intended Fleshy people to manage the rest of us instead of taking a hand at the "heavy work." She made them work averse and then made them so likable that they can usually get the rest of us to do their hard work for them.

The World Managed by Fleshy People

When he is brainy, the Fleshy man never stays in the lower ranks of subordinates. He may get a late start in an organization but he will soon make those *over* him like him so much that they will promote him to a supervisor, a foreman or a manager. Once there he will make those *under* him so fond of him that they will work long and hard for him.

Mike, a veteran real estate salesperson, is a combination of this Fleshy and Brainy types. He is a successful real estate salesperson. He continually is among the top performers at Century 21 Real

Estate Company. He is so good that he has other salespeople work for him. They are independent salespeople just like him. However, they like working with him so much that they will sell his listings whenever possible. Mike specializes in listing. He lists; the other salespeople sell his listings to their clients. If there are 2 identical properties, they will sell Mike's listing because they prefer to work with him. He just concentrates on getting listings. His conversion rate for listing appointment is close to 100%. His clients like and trust him. The other salespeople like and trust him.

The Fleshy Men to the Top

In this way, the Fleshy man with brain goes straight to the top while others look on and bewail the fact that they do most of the actual work. They fail to recognize that the world always pays the big salaries not for hand work but for head work, and not so much for working yourself as for your ability to get others to work.

The Popular Politician

This capacity for winning others is what enables this type to succeed so well in politics. The Fleshy man knows how to get votes. He mixes with everybody, jokes with everybody, remembers to ask how the children are—and pretty soon he's the representative for his constituents. Many of a big political boss is the Fleshy type with brains.

Makes Others Work

One man is but one man and at best can do little more than a good day worth of work. But a man who can induce a dozen other man-machines to speed up and turn out a full day's work apiece doesn't need to work with his own hands. He serves his employer more valuably as an overseer, foreman or supervisor.

Mike, the real estate salesperson from above example, realizes that he needs others to help him sell his listings. He alone cannot do the work of 5, 6, or 10 people. He treats the other salespeople like his clients so well that they voluntarily work for him to help him succeed at his job.

The Fleshy Salesman

If you picture a good salesman, you most likely see an image of a fleshy, round, jolly, good natured, pretty clever man whom everybody likes. For the Fleshy men are "born salesmen" and they make up a large percentage of that profession. Salesmanship requires mentality plus a pleasing personality. The Fleshy man qualifies easily in the matter of personality. Then he makes little or much money from salesmanship depending on his mental capacity.

The Fleshy Man's Habits

"Never hurry and never worry" are the unconscious standards underlying many of the reactions of this type. If you will compile a list of the habits of any Fleshy person you will find that they are mostly the outgrowths of one or both of these motives.

Inclined to Laziness

Fleshy people's habits, being built around their points of strength and weakness, are necessarily of two kinds—the desirable and the undesirable. The worst habits of this type are those inevitable to the ease-loving and the immature-minded. Laziness is one of his most undesirable traits and can cost the Fleshy dearly.

In this country where lightning-like efficiency is at a premium, only the Fleshy man with brains can hope to keep up. The inertia caused by his digestive processes is so great that it is almost insurmountable. The heavy, lazy feeling you have after a large meal is with the Fleshy man interminably because his organism is constantly in the process of digesting large amounts of food.

Likes Comfort

Love of comfort—especially such things as warm rooms and soft beds—is so deeply imbedded in the fiber of this type. This sometimes leads the excessively corpulent person to relax into laziness and sloppiness. A Fleshy individual sometimes surprises us by his ambition and immaculateness; but such a man or woman almost always combines decided mental tendencies with his fleshiness.

Enjoys Doing Favors

The habits which endear the Fleshy person to everyone and make us forget his faults are his never-failing hospitality, kindness when you are in trouble, his calming air of contentment, his tact, good nature, and the real pleasure he seems to experience when doing you a favor. His worst faults wreak upon him far greater penalties than fall upon those who associate with him, something that cannot be said of the faults of some other types.

The Babies of the Race

The first stage in biological evolution was the stage in which the digestive apparatus was developed. Processing nutrients was the first function of all life and it is the principal requirement for self-preservation. Being the first and most elemental of our five physiological systems the Fleshy—when it surpasses the others—produces a more elemental, infantile nature. The pure Fleshy has rightly been called "the baby of the race." This accounts for many of the characteristics of the extremely fleshy person, including the fact that it is difficult for him to amuse himself. He of all types likes most to be amused and very simple toys and activities are sufficient to do it.

Not Strenuous

Anything, to be popular with the Fleshy, must be easy to get, easy to do, easy to get away from, easy to drop if he feels like it. Anything requiring the expenditure of great energy, even though it promises pleasure when achieved, is usually passed over by the fleshy people.

The Art of Getting Out Of It

"Let George do it" is another bit of slang invented by this type. He seldom does anything he really hates to do. He is so likable he either induces you to let him out of it or gets somebody to do it for him. He just naturally avoids everything that is intense, difficult or strenuous.

The Peace-Loving Type

If an unpleasant situation of a personal or social nature arises—a quarrel, a misunderstanding or any kind of disagreement—the fleshy man will try to get himself out of it without a discussion. Except when they have square faces (in which case they are not pure

Fleshy), extremely fleshy people do not mix up in neighborhood, family, church, club or political quarrels. It is too much trouble, for one thing, and for another it is opposed to his peace-loving, relaxed nature.

Avoids Expensive Quarrels

The Fleshy man has his eye on personal advantages and promotions and he knows that quarrels are expensive, headache-causing, and jeopardizing his peace of mind. The Fleshy man knows instinctively that peace times are the most profitable times and though he is not for "peace at any cost" as far as the country is concerned, he certainly is much inclined that to the peaceful way where he is personally concerned. You will be amused to notice how this peace-loving quality increases as one's weight increases. The fleshier any individual is, the more is he inclined to get what he wants without hostility.

The Real Thing

The favorite "good time" of the Fleshy is one where there are plenty of refreshments. A dinner invitation always makes a hit with him, but beware that you do not lure a fleshy person into your home and give him a tea-with-lemon wisp where he expected a full meal!

Always Ready for Food

Substantial food can be served to him any hour of the day or night with the certainty of pleasing him. He loves a banquet, *provided he is not expected to make a speech*. The Fleshy man has a harder time than any other listening to long speeches. The fashion of trying to mix the two most opposite extremes—food and ideas—and expecting them to go down, was due to our misunderstanding of the real nature of human beings.

The Personal Element

Due to his immaturity, the Fleshy person gives little thought to anything except those things which affect him personally.

The calm exterior, unruffled countenance and air of deliberation he sometimes wears, and which have occasionally passed for "judicial" qualities, are largely the results of the fact that the Fleshy refuses to get stirred up over anything that does not concern him personally.

This personal element will be found to dominate the activities, conversation and interests of the Fleshy man. For him, to like a thing or buy a thing, it must come pretty near being something he can eat, wear, live in or otherwise personally enjoy. He confines himself to the concrete and tangible. But most of all, he confines himself to things out of which he gets some uses for himself.

Naturally Realistic

The Fleshy man has the child's natural innocence and ignorance of subtle and elusive things. He has the same interest in things and people as does the child, the child's indifference to books, lectures, schools and everything abstract.

Social Assets

Sweetness of disposition is one of the most valuable of all human characteristics. Fleshy people possess it more often and more unchangingly than any other type. Other social assets of this type are likeability, affability, hospitality.

Social Liabilities

Gaining his ends by flattery, cajoling, and various more or less innocent little deceptions are the only social handicaps of this type.

Emotional Assets

His unfailing optimism is the most noticeable emotional quality of this type. Nothing can be so dark that the Fleshy person doesn't find a silver lining somewhere. So, in disaster we always send for our Fleshy friends. In the presence of an amply-proportioned individual everything looks brighter. Hope springs eternal in human breasts but the springs are stronger in the plump folks than in the rest of us. Money spending is also a pronounced feature of the Fleshy man. His emotions are out-going, never "in-growing." A stingy Fleshy man is unknown.

Emotional Liabilities

A tendency to become spoiled, to pout, and to take out his resentments in babyish ways are the emotional weaknesses of this type. These, as you will note, are the natural reactions of childhood, from which he never fully emerges.

Business Assets

The ability to make people like him is the greatest business and professional asset of this type, and one every other type should emulate. One average-minded Fleshy person near the door of a business establishment will make more customers in a month by her/his geniality, joviality and sociability than a dozen brilliant thinkers will in a year. Every business that deals directly with the public should have at least one Fleshy person in it.

Business Liabilities

A habit of evading responsibility and of "getting out from under" constitutes the inclination most harmful to the business or professional ambitions of this type. Again, it is the child in him trying to escape the task set for it and at the same time to avoid punishment.

Strong Points

Optimism, hospitality and harmony are the strong points in the Fleshy man's nature. Upon them many a man has built a successful life. Without them no individual of any type can hope to be happy. His popularity and all-around compatibility give the Fleshy man advantages over other types which fairly compensate for the weak cogs in his machinery.

Weak Points

Self-indulgence of all kinds, over-eating, over-sleeping, under-exercising, and the evasion of responsibilities are the weak points of this type. Despite his many strong points, his life is often wrecked on these rocks. He so constantly tends to take the easy way out. Day by day he gives up chances for ultimate success for the baubles of immediate ease. He is the most likable of all the types but his laziness sometimes strains even the love of his family to the breaking point.

How to Deal with this Type Socially

Homo sapiens Alphabet

Feed him, give him comfortable chairs—the largest you have—and don't drag him into long discussions of any kind. This is the recipe for winning the Fleshy man when you meet him socially. And whatever you do, don't tell him your troubles! The Fleshy man hates trouble. Smothering him, you only make him ill at ease when you ply him with yours. Don't walk him any more than is absolutely necessary. Let him go home early. He enjoys his sleep and doesn't like to have it interfered with.

Make your conversation deal with concrete personal things and current events. Stay away from highbrow subjects. The best places to eat and the best shows or movies of the week are safe subjects to introduce when with extreme Fleshy people.

How to Deal with this Type in Business

Don't give him hard manual tasks. If you want this kind of work done, get someone other than an extreme Fleshy man to do it. If you hire a Fleshy man, blame yourself for the result. Give your Fleshy employee a chance to deal with people in a not-too-serious way; but hold him strictly to the keeping of his records, reports and working hours. If this Fleshy person is a dealer, a merchant, keep him to his word. Start out by letting him know you expect the delivery of just what he promises. Don't let him "jolly" you into relinquishing what is rightfully yours. And keep in mind always that the Fleshy person is usually good at heart.

Remember, the chief distinguishing marks of the Fleshy in the order of their importance are ROUNDED OUTLINES, YOUTHFUL FEATURES and DIMPLED HANDS. A person who has these is largely of the Fleshy type, no matter what other types may be included in his makeup.

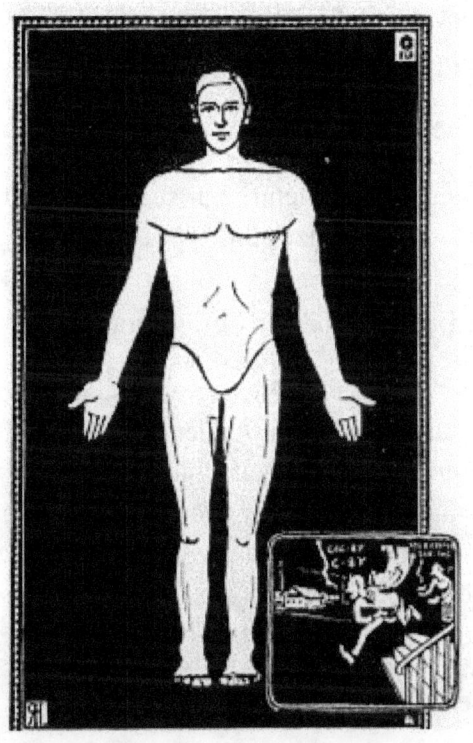

CHAPTER II

THE FLUSHED TYPE

"The Thriller"

Individual in whom the circulatory system (heart, arteries and blood vessels) and the respiratory system (lungs, nose and chest) are more highly developed than any other systems, have been named the Flushed. This name comes from the fact that the heart and lungs (which constitute the most important organs of these two closely-allied systems) are housed in the thorax—that little room made by your ribs for the protection of these vital organs.

Physical Resilience

A general elasticity of structure, a suggestion of strengths and physical resilience characterizes this type.

The Rudy-Faced, High-Chested Individual

What is known as a "red face," when accompanied by a high chest, always signifies largely Flushed tendencies. The red color which in an adult comes and goes is a sure indication of a well-developed circulatory system, since red color is caused by the rapid pumping of blood to the tiny blood vessels of the face. People with little blood, weak hearts or deficient circulation are not rosy-faced and must be much overheated or excited to show vivid color in their cheeks.

Betray Their Feelings

On the other hand, the slightest displeasure, enjoyment, surprise or exertion brings the blood rushing to the face and neck of him who has a large, well-developed blood-system. How many times you have heard such a one say: "I am so embarrassed! I flush at every little thing! How I envy the rest of you who come in from a long walk looking so cool!"

The Man of Great Chest Expansion

The largest part of this man's body is around the chest. His chest is high for the reason that he has larger lungs than the average.

Advantages of a High Chest

The man of unusual chest-expansion has one great physical asset. The person who breathes deeply has a decided advantage over the man who breathes deficiently. The lungs form the bellows or air-supply for the body's engine, the heart, and with a deficient supply of air the heart does deficient work. Efficient breathing is easy only to the man of large lungs, and only the high chested have large lungs.

Long-Waisted People

A long waist is another Flushed type's sign, for it is a natural result of the extra house-room required by the large lungs and heart. It is easily detected in both men and women. If you are a close observer you have noticed that some people appear to have a waist line much lower than others; that the belt line dividing the upper part of the body from the lower is proportionately much nearer the floor in some than in others of the same height.

In women this long waist and high chest give the appearance of small hips and of shoulders a little broader than the average; in men it gives that straight, soldier-like bearing which makes this type of man admired and gazed after as he strides down the street.

The Pure "Flushed" Head

A high head is a significant characteristic of the typical Flushed. The Anglo-Saxons tend to have this head and, more than any other races, exhibit Flushed qualities as racial characteristics. This is considered the handsomest head known. Certainly it lends the appearance of nobility and intelligence. It is not wide, looked at from the front or back, but inclines to be slightly narrower for its height than the Fleshy head.

The Kite-Shaped Face

A face widest through the cheek bones and tapering slightly up the sides of the forehead and downward to the jaw bones is the face of the pure Flushed. This must not be mistaken for the pointed chin or the pointed head, but is merely a sloping of the face upward and downward from the cheek bones as a result of the unusual width of the nose section.

His Well-Developed Nose

The nose section is also high and wide because the typical Flushed has a nose that is well developed. This is shown not only by its length but also by its high bridge.

 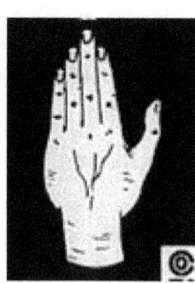

Typical Facial Features and Hand of the Flushed Type.

The cause for the width and length of this section is obvious. The nose constitutes the entrance and exit departments of the breathing system. Large lung capacity necessitates a large chamber for the intake and expulsion of air.

Signs of Good Lungs

Whenever you see a man whose face is wide through the cheek bones—with a long, high-bridged open-nostril nose—you see a man of good lung capacity and of quick physical energy. When you see any one with pinched nostrils, a face that is narrow through the cheek bones and a low or "sway-back" nose, you see a man whose lung capacity is deficient. Such a person invariably expends his physical energy more slowly. Freckles, being due to the same causes as red hair and red color, are further indications of Flushed tendencies, though you may belong to this type with or without them.

The Typical Flushed Hand

The pointed hand is the hand of the pure Flushed type. Note the extreme length of the second finger and the pointed effect of this hand when all the fingers are laid together. Any person with a pointed hand such as this has good flushed development whether it occupies first place in his makeup or not. The fingers of the Flushed are also inclined to be more thin-skinned than those of other types.

One may be a predominantly Flushed type without these elements but they are indications of the extreme Flushed type. Naturally the hand of the extreme Flushed is more pinkish than the average.

The Beautiful Foot

The Flushed tends to have narrower, high-arched feet than other types.

The Man of Energetic Movements

A hair-trigger nimbleness goes with this type. He is always "poised ready to strike." All Flushed men use their hands, arms, wrists, limbs and feet alertly and energetically. They open doors, handle tools and all kinds of hand instruments with little blundering. Also their movements are more graceful than those of other types. They talk with their hands.

The Flushed Walk

"The springy step" must have been invented to describe the walk of the Flushed person. No matter how hurried, his walk has more grace than the walk of other types. He does not stumble and it is seldom that the Flushed man steps on his partner's toes when dancing.

The Graceful Sitter

The way you sit tells a great deal about your nature. One of the first secrets it betrays is whether you are by nature graceful or ungainly. The person who sits gracefully, who seems to drape himself becomingly upon a chair and to arise from it with ease is usually a Flushed. Their excess of energy sometimes gives them the appearance of "fidgeting," but it is an easy, graceful fidget and not as disturbing as that of other types.

Keen Eye and Ear Senses

Quick eyes and keen ears are characteristic of the Flushed. The millions of stimuli—the sounds, sights and smells impinging every waking moment upon the human consciousness—affect him more quickly and more intensely than any other type. The acuteness of all our senses depends, to a far greater extent than we have previously supposed, upon proper heart and lung action. Take long, deep breaths for five minutes in the open air while walking rapidly enough to make your heart pound, and see how much keener your senses are at the end of that time. The Flushed is chronically in this condition because his heart and lungs are going at top speed habitually and naturally all his life.

The High-Strung

Nerves as taut as a violin string—due to his acute physical senses and his thin, sensitive skin—plus his instantaneous quickness make the Flushed what is known as "high-strung."

The Most Temperamental

Because he is keyed to high C by nature, the Flushed has more of that quality called temperament than any other type. The wag who said that "temperament was mostly temper" might have reversed it and still have been right. For temper is largely a matter of temperament. Since the Flushed have more "temperament" it follows naturally that they have more temper, or rather that they show it more often, just as they show their delightful qualities more often.

A Continuous Performance

This type, consciously and unconsciously, is a "continuous performance." He is showing you something of himself every moment and if you are interested in human nature, as your reading of this book suggests, you are going to find him a fascinating subject.

He is expressing his feelings with more or less abandon all the time and he is likely to express as many as a dozen different ones in as many moments.

The Quick Temper

"Flying off the handle," and "going up in the air" are phrases originally inspired by our dear, delightful friends, the Flushed. Other types do these more or less temperamental things but they do not do them as frequently nor on as short notice as this type.

The Human Firecracker

A fiery nature is entrenched in the Flushed man's makeup. But did you ever see a fiery-natured man who didn't have lots of warm friends! It is the grumpy man—in whom the fire starts slowly and smolders indefinitely—that nobody likes. But the man who flares up, flames for a moment and is calm the next never lacks for companions or devotees.

The Red-Haired

One may belong to the Flushed type whether his hair is blonde or brunette or any of the shades between, but it is an interesting fact that most of the red-haired are largely of this type. "He didn't have red hair for nothing" is a famous phrase that has been applied to the red-haired, quick-tempered Flushed for generations. You will be interested to note that this high color and high chest are distinctly noticeable in most of the red-haired people you know—certain proof that they approximate this type.

As you walk down the street tomorrow look at the people ahead of you and when you find a "red-head" notice how much more red his neck is than the necks of the people walking beside him. This red skin almost always accompanies red hair, showing that most red-haired people belong to this type.

The "Flash in the Pan"

The red-haired man's temper usually expends itself instantly. His red-hot fieriness is over in a moment. But for every enemy he has two friends—friends who like his flame, even though in constant danger from it themselves. Whereas the Fleshy avoids you if he disagrees with you, the Flushed likes to tell you in a few hot words just what he thinks of you. But the chances are that he will be so completely over it by lunch time that he will invite you out with him.

Desire for Praise

To be admired and a wee bit envied are desires dear to the heart of this type. Everybody, to a greater or lesser degree, desires these things, but to no other type do they mean so much as to this one. We know this because no other type, in any such numbers, takes the trouble or makes the sacrifices necessary to bring them about.

Shines in Public Life

The lime-light appeals more to this type than to others because it goes further toward gratifying his desire for acclaim. So while other men and women are dreaming of fame, the Flushed practices, plows, and pleads his way to it. The personal adoration of friends and of the crowd is the breath of life to him. Extremes of this type consider no self-denial too great a price to pay for it.

Many on the Stage

The stage in all its forms is as natural a field to the Flushed as salesmanship is to the Fleshy. The pleas of loving papas and fearsome mamas are usually ineffective with this type of boy or girl when he sets his heart on a career in theater or in the movies. Whether they achieve it or not will depend on other traits, chiefly mental, in each individual's makeup; but the yearning for it, in some form, is always there. So the casting company's waiting rooms are always crowded with people of this type. It is this intensity of desire which has motivated and inspired most stage artists onto success in their chosen fields.

"Instant Empathy"

To be able to put one's self in the shoes of another, to feel as he feels, to be keenly sensitive to his situation and psychology that one almost becomes that person for the time being, is the heart and soul of acting. The Flushed person has this sensitivity naturally. After a long period acquainting and observing, you may be able to put yourself in the place of a few friends. The Flushed person does this instantly and automatically.

Predisposition, Not Hard Work, Makes Fame

Those who have succeeded to fame in any given line are inclined to proclaim, "Hard work is the secret of success," and to take great credit unto themselves for the labor they have expended on their own. It is true of course that all success entails hard work. But the man or woman sufficiently gifted to rise to the heights gets from that gift such a strong inward urge towards its expression that what he does in that direction is not considered work for him. The long hours, concentration and study devoted to it are more pleasurable than painful to him. He chooses such activities voluntarily.

Nature the Real Artist

Nothing can rightly be called work which one does out of sheer preference. Work never made an actress and work never made a singer where innate talent for these arts was lacking. Nature, the true maker of every famous name, bestows ninety per cent and man, if he hustles, can provide the other very necessary ten.

Success for All

Every individual who is not feeble-minded can be a success at something in this big world. Every normal-minded individual is able to create, invent, improve, organize, build or market some of the myriads of things the world is crying for. But he will succeed at only those things in which his physiological and psychological mechanisms perform their functions easily and naturally.

Why We Work

Man is, by inclination, very little of a worker. He is, first, a wanter—a bundle of instincts, second, a feeler—a bundle of emotions, last and least, he is a thinker. What real work he does is done not because he truly likes it but because it serves one of these first two bundles. When the desire for leisure is stronger than the other urges, leisure wins. But in all ambitious men and women the desire for other things outweighs the leisure urge.

Ambition and the Flushed Type

Now what is it that causes some to have ambition and others to lack it? Your ambitions take the form determined by your predominating physiological system. For instance, in every great singer the Flushed trait has been present either as the first or second element. The effect of the physical traits upon our talents is no more noticeable anywhere than here. For it is his unusual lung power, his high chest, the sounding boards in his nose section and his superior vocal cords that make the real foundation of every singer's fame. These physiological conditions are found in extreme degree only in persons of Flushed tendencies. The nature resulting from a large heart and large lungs is one distinctly different from all others—in short, the Flushed nature.

The Best Dressed

The best dressed man and the best dressed woman in your town belong predominantly to this type. This is no accident. The Flushed, being possessed of acute eye senses, are more sensitive to color, shape, and line than any other type. These are the foundations of "style" and artistic grooming.

Clothes Can Unmake the Man

Being desirous of the praise of others and realizing that though clothes do not make the man they can unmake him, this type looks to his laurels on this point. Because clothes determine the first impressions we make upon strangers and because that impression is difficult to change, clothes are of vast importance in this maze of human relationships.

The Flushed is more sensitive to the attitude of others because their attitude is more vital to his self-expression. He senses from childhood the bearing that clothes have for or against him in the opinion of others and how they can aid him to express his personality.

Distinction in Dress

The distinctive dresser is one who painstakingly chooses the appropriately fashionable wardrobe for the occasion and never forgets the "last moment" touch. He is always a step or two ahead of the times. His clothes are "up to the minute." Such a man or woman invariably has a large Flushed development and is well repaid by the public for his pains.

Dress the Universal Language

The public looks eagerly to the new trend in fashion styles every season. It gives the men or women instantaneous admiration for staying on top of new fashion. This being one of the quickest roads to praise, it is often utilized by this type.

Always on "Fashion Parade"

With intent to keep the spotlight on him or her, the Flushed is always on fashion parade. He is vividly aware of himself. He knows what kind of picture he is making. He is seldom "self-conscious," in the sense of being timid. When he does happen to be timid he suffers, by reason of his greater desire for approval, more acutely than any other type.

Cocked Gun His Keynote

Instantaneous reaction to stimuli—with all the reflex actions resulting therefrom—constitutes the keynote of this type. This makes an individual who is: shoot, aim, and ready. Because life is full of all kinds of stimuli, acting during every waking moment upon every sense in the organism, any person who is high strung finds himself in the midst of what might be called "nerve-madhouse."

Gets the Most Out of Everything

Because of this same highly sensitized makeup, the Flushed type gets more sensations out of every incident than the rest of us do. He experiences more joy in the space of a lifetime but also more disappointment.

The Human Violin

For the same reason that the violin vibrates to a greater number of sounds than the organ, the Flushed is a more vibrant individual than others. He is impelled to an expressiveness of voice, manner and action that often looks like pretense to less impulsive people. In other types it would be, but to the Flushed it is so natural and normal that he is often much surprised to hear that he has the reputation of being "pretentious."

A Reputation for Flightiness

This lightning-like liveliness of face, body and voice, his quick replies and instantaneous reactions to everything also cause him to be called "flighty."

The Quick Thinker

Homo sapiens Alphabet

We are prone to judge every one by ourselves. People, whose mental or physical senses are less keen and less sensitive, call the Flushed man "rattle-brained." Usually such a man's brain is not rattled at all. It is working, as all brains do in response to the messages reaching it, via the wires of the five senses.

In the Flushed man, these wires transmit information much quicker than in the other types. He gets sensations from sights, sounds, tastes, touches and smells much more quickly than the rest of us do. These messages are sent to the brain more rapidly; and since sensation is responsible for much of our thinking, this man's brain thinks a little more speedily than that of other types.

It does not necessarily think any better. Often it does need slowing down. But compared to the thought-power of some of the other types the Flushed man's speed makes up for much of his carelessness. He makes more mistakes in judgment than other types but can amend so quickly. He usually remedies them while other types are still trying to decide when to start. To hold himself back is the hardest lesson for this type to learn.

Vacillation

This tendency to let himself go brings the Flushed man a great deal of unhappiness and failure. He plunges so quickly that he often fails to take into consideration the various elements of the situation. His physical senses tell him a thing should be done and rush headlong into actions that he knows are ill-advised the moment he has time to think them over. In turning around and righting his mistakes he often hears him being called "changeable" and "vacillating."

His "Batting Average"

In this, as in other things, we have a tendency toward smugness, shortsightedness and egotism. The man who makes but one mistake a year because he makes but two decisions is wrong fifty per cent of the time. Yet he satisfactorily considers himself superior to the Flushed person because the Flushed got in six "poor deals within six months." At the rate the average Flushed man acts, this would be about one mistake in a thousand—a much "better batting average" than the other man's.

But because the confidence of others in our stability is of prime importance to us all, this type or any one inclined to definite Flushed tendencies should take pains to prevent this impression from settling into the minds of his friends.

Usually Slightly Thrilled

Even when apparently composed the Flushed is always a wee bit thrilled. Everything he sees, hears, touches, tastes or smells gives him such keen sensations that he lives momentarily in some kind of adventure. He languishes in an unchanging environment and finds monotony almost unbearable.

Continually stimulated senses

"Never two minutes the same" fitly describes this type. He passes rapidly from one vivid sensation to another and expresses each one so completely that he is soon ready for the next. He has fewer complexes than any other type because he does not inhibit as much.

The Uncorked Bottle

The "lid" is always off of the Flushed man. This being the case he suffers little from "mental congestion" though he sometimes pays a high price for his self-expression. How many marriage proposals have been made in the cloudy haze of passion that was regretted later?

Everybody is Interesting

Most of us are much more interesting than the world suspects. But the world is not made up of mind readers. We keep our most interesting thoughts and the most interesting side of ourselves hidden away. Even your dearest friends are seldom given a peep into the actual You. And this despite the fact that we all recognize this as a deficiency in others.

We bottle up ourselves and defy the world's cork-screws—all except the Flushed. He allows his associates to see much of what is passing in his mind all the time. Because we are all interested in the real individual and not in masks this type usually is much sought after.

Not Secretive

The Flushed man does not, by preference, cover up. He does not, by preference, secretive. He does not, except when necessary, keep his plans and practice private. He is likely to tell not only his family but his newest acquaintances just what he is planning to do and how he expects to do it. The naturally secretive person who vaguely refers to "a certain party" when he has occasion to speak of another is the exact opposite of this type.

Naturally Charming

Homo sapiens Alphabet

Personal experiences, personal secrets and personal preferences are subjects we are all interested in. These are the very things with which the Flushed delights his friends and about which he is more frank and outspoken than any other type. He makes many friends by his obvious openness and his capacity for seeing the interesting details which others overlook.

Charming Conversationalist

Colorful, vivid words and phrases come easily to the tongue of this type because he sees the unusual, the fascinating, in everything. Since anyone can make a thing interesting to others if he is really interested in it himself, the Flushed makes others see and feel what he describes. He is therefore known as the most charming conversationalist.

Beautiful Voice

The most beautiful voices belong to people who are largely of this type. This is due, as we have said before, to physiological causes. The high chest, sensitive vocal cords, spacious sounding boards in the nose and roof of the mouth all tend to give the voice of the Flushed many nuances and accents never found in other types.

His pleasing voice plus the vividness of his expressions and his boldness in giving the intimate and interesting details are other traits which help to make the Flushed a lively companion.

The Lure of Spontaneity

The most beloved people in the world are the spontaneous. We lead such drab lives ourselves and hold back so much; we like to see a little Niagara Fall of human emotion occasionally. The Flushed person feels everything keenly. Life's experiences make vivid records on the sensitive plate of his mind. He puts them on the Big Screen that is himself and proceeds to run them off for your entertainment.

I backpacked through Southeast Asia for many months right after getting my MBA and the pesky resulting debt. I again quit a real estate career while at the height of the market to start a language school for kids in Vietnam. I am predominantly this Flushed type. Understanding my physical traits, my behaviors are easily understood.

The Loquacious

"That person's talk gets on my nerves," is a remark often made by one of the staid, stiff types concerning the seldom silent, extreme Flushed individual. So natural is this to the Flushed that he is entirely unconscious of the wearisome effect he has on other people.

A Sense of Humor

Seeing the funny side of everything is a capacity which comes more naturally to this type than to others. Real humor lies in detecting and describing that intangible quirk. No type has the insightfulness essential to this in such high degree as the Flushed. Individuals of other types sometimes possess a keen sense of humor. This trait is not confined to the Flushed; but it is a significant fact that almost every well-known humorist has had this type as the first or second element in his makeup.

The Human Firecrackers

"He is animated," or "she is a firecracker," are phrases often used to describe that vivacious individual whose adeptness at repartee puts the rest of the crowd in the background. These people are always largely or pure Flushed. They never belong predominately to the fourth type. The next time you find such a person note how his eyes flash, how his color comes and goes and the many indescribable gradations of voice which make him the center of things. "He is always shooting sparks," said a man recently in describing a Flushed, high-chested friend.

Rarely Dull Company

His "line" may not interest you but the Flushed himself is usually interesting. He is an actual curiosity to the quiet, inexpressive people who never can fathom how he manages to talk so frankly and so fast. Such a person is seldom dull. He is everything from a condiment to a cocktail and has the same effect on the average group of more or less drab personalities.

Lives in the High and Low

"Happy one moment and sad the next" is the way the happy meter would read if it could make a record of the inner feelings of the average Flushed type. These feelings often come and go without his having the least notion of what causes them. Ordinarily these unaccountable moods are due to sensations reaching his subconscious mind, which the conscious mind is not aware of.

Called "Intuitive"

This ability to "get" things, to respond quickly with his physical reactions while devoting his mental ones to something else, has obtained for this type the reputation of possessing more "intuition" than others.

Source of "Hunches"

Some people say that "hunches' happen when supernatural being communicates through us. However, the impression that he gets this knowledge or suspicion from the outside is due, the scientists say, to the fact that his thinking was working at such lightning-like speed that he was unable to watch the wheels go round. The only thing of which he is conscious is the final result or the sum at the bottom of the column called his "hunch." He is not aware of the addition and subtraction which his mind went through to get it for him.

Easily Excited

"Off like a shot" is a term often applied to the Flushed. He is the most easily excited of all types but also the most easily calmed. He recovers from every mood more quickly and more completely than other types. Under the influence of emotion, he often does things that he is sorry immediately afterward. This has gotten many Flushed type people into real trouble.

On the Spur of the Moment

This type usually does a thing quickly or not at all. He is a gun that is always cocked. So he hits a great many things in the course of a lifetime and leads the most exciting existence of any type. Being able to get thrills out of the most ordinary event because of seeing elements in it which others overlook, he finds in everyday life more novelty than others ever see.

The Adventurers

Romance and adventure always interest this type. He lives for thrills and novel reactions and usually spares no pains or money to get them. A representative expression used frequently by these people is, "I got a real kick out of that."

This craving for adventure, suspense and zest often lures this type into speculation, gambling and various games of chance. The danger in flying, deep-sea diving, auto-racing and similar fields have a strong appeal for this type—so strong that practically every man or woman who follows these professions is of this type.

Tires of Sameness

The Flushed soon tires of the same suit, the same gown, the same house, the same town and even the same girl. He wrings the utmost out of each experience so quickly and so completely that he is forever on the lookout for new worlds to conquer. Past experiences are to him as so many lemons out of which he has taken all the juice. He anticipates the future as so many more lemons to be utilized in the same way.

Likes Responsive People

We all like answers. We want to be assured that what we have said or done has registered. The Flushed is always saying or doing something and can't understand why other people are so unresponsive. He is as responsive as a computer keyboard.

Everything hits the mark with him and he lets you know it. So, naturally, he enjoys the same from others and considers those less expressive than he stiff, formal or dull. The kind of person the Flushed likes best is one who likes him enough to nod and smile and show that he fully understands but will not interrupt his stream of talk.

People He Dislikes

The dull, indifferent, or cold are people the Flushed comes very near disliking. Their evident self-complacency and immobility are things he does not understand at all and with which he has little patience. Such people seem to him to be cold, unfeeling, and almost dead. So he steers clear of them.

The Forgiving Man

If you have once been a real friend of a Flushed and a quarrel comes between you, he may be so bitter and biting in the moment of his anger but in most cases he will forgive you eventually.

Really Forgets Disagreements

It is not as easy for other types to forgive; they often refrain from attempting reconciliation. But the Flushed person's forgiveness is not only spontaneous but genuine. The Fleshy type bears no grudges because it is too much trouble. The Flushed man finds it hard to maintain a grudge because he gets over it just as he gets over everything else. His anger withers away or he wakes up some fine morning and finds, like the boy recovering from the chickenpox, that he "simply hasn't it anymore."

Likes Fancy Foods

Homo sapiens Alphabet

Variety and novelty in food are much enjoyed by this type. The Fleshy type likes lots of rich food but he is not so desirous of varieties or bizarre dishes, but the Flushed man specializes in them. If you mention some kind of strange interesting new dish, certainly someone in the crowd will be interested in investigating it. That person is usually the Flushed type. It gives him another promise of "newness."

The introduction of almost all foreign foods into this country depends almost entirely upon these typical Flushed patrons. Most chefs or restaurant-owners have this to say of this type, "they will try anything once."

Required Ambiance for Dinner

Out-of-the-ordinary surroundings in which to dine are always welcome to this type. The decorations, pictures on the wall, and furniture mean much to him. Most people like music at meals but to the Flushed type, it is almost indispensable. He is so alive in every nerve, keen in every sense and has such intense capacity for enjoyment of many things simultaneously that he demands more than other types. An attentive waiter who attends to every movement and anticipates every wish of patrons is also a favorite with the Flushed type when dining out.

Sensitive to His Surroundings

Colorful surroundings are more necessary to the Flushed type than to others. The ever-changing fashions in house decorations are welcome innovations to him. He soon grows tired of anything regardless of how much he liked it to begin with.

Take notice amongst your friends and you will see that the women who change the furniture all around every few weeks are invariably of this type. "It makes me feel that I have changed my location and takes the place of a trip," explained one girl not long ago.

Wants "Something Different"

The exact color of curtains, wall-paper, interior decorations and accessories are matters of vital import to this type. Whereas the Fleshy type demand comfort, the Flushed one asks for "something different," something that catches and holds the eye—that makes an instantaneous impression upon the spectator and gives him one more thing by which to remember the personality of the one who lives there. This type considers his room and home as a part of himself and takes the pains with them which he bestows upon his clothes.

When He is Rich

Wealth to the Flushed type means unlimited opportunity for achieving the unusual in everything. His tastes are more extravagant than those of other types. Uncommon works of art are usually found in the homes of this type. The most extraordinary things from the most extraordinary places are special preferences with him. He carries out his desire for attention here as in everything else and what he buys will serve that end directly or indirectly.

Fashion and "Flare"

"Flare" aptly describes the quality which the pure Flushed man desires in all that touches him and his personality. It must have vitality and panache and distinction. It must be "the latest" and "chic." He is the last type of all to submit to wearing last year's suit, singing last year's songs, or driving in a last year's model.

Likes Dash

The Flushed man wants everything he wears, drives, lives in or owns to "impress". The Fleshy man loves comfort above all else, but the Flushed man loves distinction. He does not demand such easy-to-wear garments as the Fleshy man. On the contrary, he will undergo extreme discomfort if it gives him a distinctive appearance. He wants his house to be elegant, the yard "different," the view unusual.

Has Color Sense

When the Fleshy man furnishes a home, he devotes his attention to soft beds, coziness, and plenty of cushioned sofas, while the Flushed one thinks of the chandeliers, the unusual chairs, the impressive front doorstep, the landscape gardening and the color schemes.

When He is in Moderate Circumstances

When only well-to-do, this type will be found to have carried out furnishings and decorations with the taste worthy of much larger purses. When merely well-to-do, he wears the very best clothes he can possibly afford, and often a good deal better. This type does not intend to be outwitted by life. He tries always to put up a good front.

When He is Poor

The Flushed is seldom poor. He has so much personality, flair, and energy that are required in today's world that he usually has a good position. He may not like the position. But in spite of the fact that he finds it harder to tolerate disagreeable things than any other type, he will endure it for he knows that the rewards he is after cannot be had by the empty pocket.

The World Entertained by Them

On stage, you will find more people of this type than any other. The Fleshy type manages the world but the Flushed one entertains it. He comprises more of the dancers, actors, singers, comedians, and general entertainers than any other two types combined. In everything except acrobatics and oratory he holds the platform of glories. As already pointed out, his adaptability, spontaneity and love of admiration are responsible for this.

His Fastidious Habits

The Flushed man is the most fastidious of all the types. His thin skin and sensitive nerves make him more conscious of roughness and sloppiness than others. The result is that he is what is called "more particular" about his person than are other types. The Fleshy man often wears an old pair of shoes long past their usefulness, but the Flushed man or woman thinks more of the impression he creates than of his own personal comfort, and will wear the shiniest leathers on the hottest day if they are the best match for his suit.

Social Assets

Charm and responsiveness are the chief social assets of the Flushed type. Inasmuch as these are the most valuable of all social traits, he has a better natural start in human relationships than any other type.

Social Liabilities

Quick temper, inflammable nature and appearances of vanity are this type's great social liabilities. They stand between him and success many times. He must learn to control them if he desires to reap the full benefit of his remarkable assets.

Emotional Assets

Instantaneous sympathy and the lack of poisonous inhibitions are the outstanding emotional assets of this type.

Emotional Liabilities

Impatience, mercurial emotions and the expenditure of too much of his electricity in every little experience are the tendencies most to be guarded against.

Business Assets

He is a "good mixer" and has the magnetism to interest and attract others are his valuable business traits.

Business Liabilities

An appearance of flightiness and his tendency to hop from one subject to another, stand in the way of the Flushed man's promotion many times.

Strong Points

Personal ambition, adaptability and quick physical energy are the strong points of the Flushed type.

Weak Points

Excitability, irresponsibility, and ultra-sensitivity, are the weak points of this type.

How to Deal with This Type Socially

Give him esthetic surroundings, encourage him to talk, and respond to what he says. These are the certain methods for winning him in social intercourse.

How to Deal with this Type in Business

Get his name on the dotted line NOW, or don't expect it. If he is an employee let him come into direct contact with people, give his personality a chance to get business for you, don't forget to praise him when deserved, and don't pin him down to routine. This type succeeds best in professions where his personal charm can be capitalized.

Remember, the chief distinguishing marks of the Flushed type in the order of their importance, are FLUSHED COMPLEXION, HIGH CHEST and LONG WAIST. Any person who has these is largely of the Flushed type, no matter what other types may be included in his makeup.

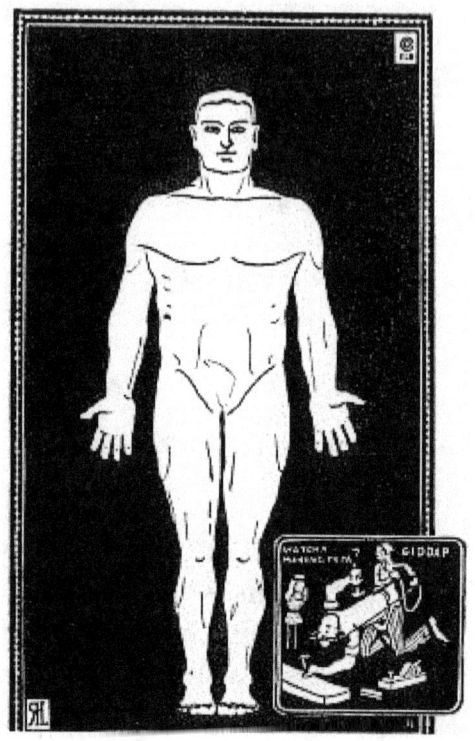

CHAPTER III

THE MUSCULAR TYPE

"The Worker"

People in whom the muscular system is proportionately larger and more highly developed than any of their other systems are Muscular. This system consists of the muscles of the organism.

The "Lean Meat" Type

Homo sapiens Alphabet

The muscle-system of the human body is simply a coordinated, organized arrangement of layers of lean meat, of which every individual has a complete set. An individual's muscles may be small, flabby, deficient in strength or so thin as to be almost imperceptible but they are always there—elementary in the infant, full grown in the adult and remnants in the aged. But they are so smoothly fitted together, so closely knitted and usually so well covered that we seldom realize their complexity or importance.

In the pure Muscular type his muscles are firm and large. Such muscles cannot be disguised but seem to stand out all over him.

Helpless Without Them

Without them we would be helpless masses of flesh and bone; we could not blink an eye or lift a finger. Yet we are so accustomed to them that we rarely think of them and seldom give them credit for what they do.

Without their wonder-work to adjust the eyes we could not see; without their power the heart would cease to beat. We cannot smile, sob, speak or sing without using them. We would have no pianists, violinists, dancers, aviators, inventors or workers of any kind without them.

Everything we build—from patio to skyscrapers—is planned by our brains but depends for its realization upon the muscles of the human body.

How to Know Him

Homo sapiens Alphabet

Look at any individual and you will note one of these three conditions: that his bones seem to be covered just by skin and muscles (which means that he belongs to the Bony type) or thickly padded with flesh (in which case he is largely of the Fleshy type) or well upholstered with *firm* meat. In the latter case he is largely Muscular, no matter what other types may be present in his makeup.

In a short time you will be able to tell, at a glance, whether the padding on an individual is mostly flesh or mostly muscle, because flesh is always round and soft while muscle is firm and definite.

Physical Solidity

A general solidity of structure, as distinguished from the softness of the Fleshy type and the resilience of the Flushed type, characterizes the Muscular. Poke your finger into a Fleshy man's hand and though it makes a dent that dent puffs back quickly. Do the same to the Muscular and you will find a firmness and toughness of fiber that resists but stays there longer once the dent is made.

Not So Malleable

This little illustration is typical of the differences between these two natures throughout their entirety. Just as the Fleshy man's face gives to your touch, *he* will give in to you more easily than any other type; but he will go back to the same place sooner and more smoothly when your pressure is removed.

The Muscular type does not mold so easily, is less suggestible, is less tractable than the Fleshy or Flushed one, but is less likely to revert afterwards.

Homo sapiens Alphabet

Built on the Square

"On the Square" is a figurative expression usually applying to a moral tendency. In this sense it is as often possessed by one type as another. But in a purely literal sense the Muscular is actually built on the square. His whole figure is a combination of squares.

The Fleshy type is built upon the circle, the Flushed on the kite-shape but the pure Muscular always tends toward a squareness of outline.

We repeat, he is no more "square" morally than any other type, so do not make the mistake of attributing any more of this virtue to him than to others.

Each type has its own weaknesses and points of strength as different from other types and these are responsible for most of the moral differences between people.

The Tree Trunk

The extreme Muscular type is below medium height, though one of any height may be largely muscular. The extreme type, of which we are treating in this chapter, is shorter and heavier than the average. But his heaviness is due to *muscle* instead of flesh. He has the appearance of standing firmly, solidly upon the ground, of being stalwart and strong.

The Square-Shouldered Man

The Muscular type's shoulders stand out more nearly at right angles than those of any other type and are much broader in proportion to his height. The Fleshy has sloping shoulders and the Flushed inclines to high shoulders. But the shoulders of the pure Muscular type are straighter and have squareness where the Fleshy man's have curves. This accounts for the fact that most of the square shouldered men you have known were not tall men, but medium or below medium in height. The wide square shoulders do not accompany any other pure type, though naturally they may be present in an individual who is a combination.

Has Proportionately Long Arms

The arms of pure Muscular are longer in proportion to the body than the arms of other types. The arms of the Fleshy are short for his body but the extreme Muscular's arms are always anywhere from slightly longer to very much longer than his height would lead you to expect.

The Pure Muscular Head

A "square head" is the first thing you think of when you look at a pure Muscular. His head has no such decided digressions from the normal as the round head of the Fleshy or the kite-shaped head of the Flushed man. It is not high for his body like the Flushed man's or small for his body like the Fleshy man's, but is of average proportions.

 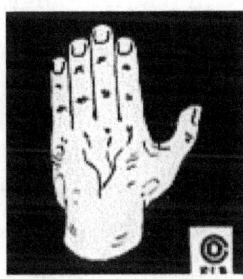

Typical Facial Features and Hand of the Muscular type

His Thick Neck

A distinctive feature of this type is his thick neck. It is not fleshy like that of the Fleshy one or medium long like that of the Flushed but has unusual muscularity and strength.

This is one of the main indications of the Muscular's strength. A sturdy neck is one of the most significant indications of physical prowess and longevity, while the frail neck—of which we shall speak in connection with the fifth type—is always a sign of the physical frailty which endangers life. The thickness of his neck may sometimes give you the impression that the Muscular head is small but if you will look again you will see that it is normal for his bodily size.

His Square Face

Looking at him from directly in front you will see that the Muscular's face gives you an impression of squareness. You will also notice that his side-head, cheeks and jaw run up and down in such a way as to give him a right-angled face.

His Square Jaw

A broad jaw is another characteristic of this type. Not only is it square, looked at from the front, but you are pretty sure to note that the jaw bones, as they proceed downward under the ear, tend to make a right-angled turn at the corners instead of a rounded curve.

These dimensions tend to give the whole lower part of the Muscular's face a box-like appearance. It is considered attractive for men but robs its female owners of the delicate, pointed chin so much desired by women.

The Typical Muscular Hand

Notice the hands of the people you meet and you will be surprised to see how different and how interesting they are. Their size, shape and structure as seen from the back of the hand are especially significant and tell us much more about the individual's nature than the palm does.

Perhaps you have thought that a hand was just a hand. But there are hands and hands. Each pure type has its own and no other is ever seen on the extreme of that type.

The hand of the Muscular, like all the rest of his body, is built in a series of squares. It runs out from the wrist and down in a straighter line and tends to right angles.

The Square Fingers of This Type

Homo sapiens Alphabet

"Spatulate fingers"—meaning fingers that are square or paddle-shaped at the tips—are sure indications of a decided muscular tendency.

He may have other types in combination but if his fingers are really square—"sawed off at the ends" in such a way as to give them large instead of tapering ends—that person has more than average muscularity and the activities of his life will tend in the directions referred to in this chapter.

The Manual Worker

Muscular men are the hand-workers of the world. They are the artisans, craftsmen, the constructors and builders.

We all tend to use most those organs or parts of the body which are largest and most highly developed. The Muscular's hand is proportionately larger than the hand of any other type. It has more muscle, that one element without which good hand work is impossible.

So it has followed inevitably that the manual work of the world is done largely by Muscular men. Their hands are also so much more powerful that they do not tire easily.

The Hand of the Creative Artist

"The artist's hand" and "the artistic hand" are phrases long used but misused. Delicate tapering fingers were supposed in ancient times to denote artistic ability. The frail curving hand was also supposed to be a sign of artistic talent.

Homo sapiens Alphabet

From the stage of the ancient down to the movies of today, the typical artist is pictured with a slight, slender hand. This tapering-fingered hand denotes a keen sense of artistic values, a love of the esthetic, refined and beautiful, and real artistic *appreciation*, but *not* the ability to create.

The "Hand Arts"

Before we explain this, kindly understand that we are speaking only of those arts which require hand work—and not of such arts as singing, dancing, or musical composition which could more properly be called artistic activities. We are referring only to those arts which depend for their creation upon the human hand—such as painting, architecture, craftsmanship, cartooning, sculpture, violin, piano, etc.

All these are created by square fingered people.

We are too much inclined to think of the products of these arts as being created out of sheer artistic sense, artistic taste or artistic insight. But a moment's reflection will show that every tangible artistic creation is the result of unusual hand work combined with gifted head work. Without a sure, strong, well-knit hand the ideas of the greatest artists could never have materialized. The lack of such a hand explains why the esthetic, the artistic-minded and the connoisseur do not *create* the beautiful things they *appreciate*.

Head and Hand Partners

The hand must execute what the brain plans and it must be a perfect mechanism so that it responds to the most elusive inspirations of the artist. It must be a near fifty percent partner; otherwise, its owner will never produce real art.

No type has this strong, sure, coordinated hand-machine to any such degree as the Muscular.

The fingers, which are of the utmost significance in the creation of artistic things, must be fitted with well-developed muscles of extreme efficiency or the execution will fall short of the ideal the artist pictures in his mind.

The pure Muscular type seldom makes an artist as an inspired brain is the other important element in the creation of art. This is the forte of the Brainy type. A combination of the Brainy type with the Muscular makes most artists using their hands to create. A combination of the Muscular and the Flushed type makes most singers. Most artists using hands to create will be found to have spatulate-fingered hands—in short, muscular hands.

The hand of most famous craftsmen, sculptors, and painters is usually larger and heavier than that of the average person, instead of being more frail and delicate. Such a hand is a certain indication of the muscular element in that individual's makeup.

His Powerful Movements

Forceful, decisive movements also characterize this type. He is inclined to go at even the most trivial things with as much force as if the world depended on it.

His Forceful Walk

Heavy, powerful, forceful strides distinguish the walk of this type. If he has but ten steps to go he will start off as if beginning an around-the-world marathon.

You Hear Him Coming

All Muscular types notify others of their approach by their forceful walk. They are unconscious of this loud instinctive tread, and most of them will be surprised to read it here. But their friends will recognize it. The chances are that they have often spoken of it amongst themselves.

The Loud Voice

The "thunderous voice" belongs almost always to a Muscular. He does his talking just as he does everything else—with all his might. It is very difficult for the Muscular man to "tone down" this powerful voice. His long-suffering friends will testify to this characteristic.

His Thunderous Tones

This loud voice is a serious social handicap to him. His only chance of compensation for it lies in its use before juries, congregations or large audiences. It might be noted here that every great orator has been largely of this type, and also that his fame came not alone from the things he said but from the thunderous tones in which he delivers them.

The Solid Sitter

When a Muscular man sits down, he does it as he does everything—with definiteness and force. He does not spill over as does the Fleshy or drape himself gracefully like the Flushed, but plunks himself as though he meant business.

Activity His Keynote

The Muscular is more active than any other type because he is built for it. Without muscles no organism could move itself from the spot in which it was born.

Biology teaches us that the stomach was the first thing evolved. The original one-cell organism possessed but one function—digestion. As life progressed, it became necessary to send nutrients to those parts of the organism far from the stomach.

For the purpose of reaching these suburbs, the circulatory system was developed and this gave rise to the Flushed type.

Movement and Development

As time went on movement became necessary, full development not being possible to any static organism. To meet this need, muscles were evolved and organic life began to move.

It was only a wiggle at first, but that wiggle has grown till today, it includes every kind of labor, globe-trotting and immigration. The Muscular man is fitted with the best traveling equipment of any type and invariably lives a life whose main reactions express these things.

The Immigrant Muscular

No matter what his work or play the Muscular will make more moves during the course of a day than other types. He loves action because his muscles, being over-equipped for it, keep urging him from within to do things.

As a result this type makes up most of the immigrants of the world. Italians, Poles, Irish, Greeks, Russians, Germans and Jews are largely of this type and these are the races furnishing the largest number of foreigners in America.

Dullness Irks Him

Shut up a Muscular man and you destroy him. His big muscle system cries out for something to do. He becomes restless, nervous, and ill when confined or compelled to be idle.

The Fleshy man loves an easy time but the Muscular dislikes ease except when exhausted. Even then it is almost impossible to stop him.

Must Be Doing Something

"I can't bear to be doing nothing!" you often hear people say. Such a person always has plenty of muscle. Muscular men want to feel that they are not wasting time. They must be "up and doing," accomplishing something. If there is nothing near them that needs doing they are sure to go and find something.

The Born Worker

Work is second nature to this type. He really prefers it.

Everyone likes some kind of work when in the mood if it serves a purpose or an ideal. But the Muscular likes work for its own sake— or rather for the activity's sake.

Work palls the Fleshy man and monotony palls the Flushed; but leisure is what palls the Muscular. He may have worked ten years without a vacation and he may imagine he wants a long one; but by the morning of the third day you will notice he has found a piece of work for himself. It may be nothing more than hanging the screen door, chopping the wood or dusting the furniture, but it will furnish him with some kind of activity.

Because he enjoys action for its own sake and because work is only applied action, this type makes the best worker. He can be trusted to work harder than any other type.

Require Less Watching

It is no accident that the three-hundred-men gangs of foreign workmen who dig ditches, tunnels and tubes, construct buildings, railroads and cities work with fewer foremen and supervisors than are ordinarily required to keep much smaller forces of other employees at their posts.

Seldom Unemployed

For this reason the Muscular is seldom out of work. He is in demand at the best current wages because he can be depended upon to "keep at it." If we look at the unemployed and the homeless in the US during a healthy economy, very few of them would be the Muscular type.

Likes To Do Things

Because he is such a hard worker, this type gets a good deal of praise and glory. Work is almost as pleasant to the Muscular as leisure is to the Fleshy one.

The Muscular's Aggression

Fighters—those who really enjoy a brawl occasionally—are invariably Muscular type. Their square jaws—the sure sign of great muscularity—are famous the world over and especially so in these days when war was in fashion.

Combat or personal fighting is a matter of muscle-action. Being well equipped for it, this type actually enjoys it. That is why he is in trouble more often than any other type.

Loves the Strenuous Life

"The strenuous life" was another of Theodore Roosevelt's pet phrases and came from the natural leanings of his type. The true Muscular man is naturally strenuous.

We tell others to do certain things because "it will do you good"; but the real reason usually is that we like to do it ourselves.

Durability in Clothes

Something that will wear well is what this type asks for when he drops in to buy a suit. The Muscular men are neither parsimonious nor stingy. Their buying the most durable in everything is not so much to save money as for the purpose of having something they do not need to be afraid to handle.

Likes Heavy Materials

This type likes heavy, stable materials. Whereas the Fleshy wants comfortable clothes, the Flushed distinctive ones, the Muscular wants wearable, "everyday" clothes.

He wants the materials to be of the best but he cares less for color than the Flushed. Quality rather than style and plainness rather than prettiness are his standards in clothes.

"Making over father's pants for Johnnie" is a job which Muscular women have excelled in and for which they have become famous. For this type of mother not only sees to it that father's pants are of the kind of stuff that won't wear out easily but she has the square, creative hand that enjoys construction.

The Plain Dresser

Simple dresses are the ones the Muscular woman likes. This type cares little about clothes as ornament. He is intent on getting his desires satisfied by DOING things, not by looking them. He also resents the time and trouble that fashionable dressing demands. No matter how much money this type has he will not be inclined to extremes in dress. Muscular men are not really interested in clothes for clothes' sake. It is not that this type is not ambitious. He is extremely so, but he is so concentrated on "getting things done" that he is likely to forget how he looks while doing them.

When a person of this type does take great pains with his clothes it is always for a purpose, and not because he enjoys preening himself. There is little of the peacock in the Muscular.

A Simple Soul

Muscular are the most democratic of all the types. The Flushed is a natural aristocrat, and enjoys the feeling of a little innocent superiority. But Muscular often refuse to take advantage of superior positions gained through wealth or class, and are inclined to treat everybody as an equal. It is almost impossible for this type, even though he may have become or have been born a millionaire, to "lord it over" others. He is given to backing democratic movements of all kinds. This explains why Muscular constitute the large majority in every radical group.

Humanness His Hobby

Being "human" is an ideal to which this type adheres with almost religious zeal. He likes the ordinary things and is never a follower of "the trend" though he has no prejudices against it, as the Bony type has.

An Everyday Individual

The Muscular man does not care for "show" and, except when essential to the success of his aims, seldom does anything for "appearances." He is not an easy-going companion like the Fleshy man or an entertaining one like the Flushed, but an everyday sort of person.

When in Trouble

This type is not given to sliding out of difficulties like the Fleshy or to being temporarily submerged by them like the Flushed type. He "stands up to them". When in trouble he acts, instead of merely thinking.

The Most Practical Type

Homo sapiens Alphabet

"The Pragmatist" is often used to describe this type. He is inclined to look at everything from the standpoint of its practicality and is neither stingy nor extravagant.

He Likes What Works

"Will it work?" is the question this type puts to everything. If it doesn't, though it may be the most fascinating or the most entertaining thing in the world, he will take little interest in it.

This type depends mostly upon his own hands and head to make his fortune for him, and is seldom lured into risking money on things he has not seen.

The Natural Efficiency Expert

The shortest, surest way is the one this type likes. He is not inclined to fussiness. He insists on things being done in the most efficient way and he usually does them that way himself. He is not an easy man to work for, but quick to reward merit. The Muscular man does not necessarily demand money or the things that money buys but he tries to get the workable out of life.

The Property Owner

This type likes to have a fair bank account and to give his children a worthwhile training. He is less inclined to decorate them with luxuries but he will plan years ahead for their education.

These are not rigid parents like the Bony type, or lenient like the Fleshy type, or unpredictable with their children like the Flushed type, but practical and very efficient in their parenthood. They are very fond of their children but do not "spoil" them as often as some of the other types do.

They bring up their children to work and teach them early in life how to do things. As a result, the children of this type become useful at an early age and usually know how to earn a living if necessary.

Wants the Necessities

The necessities of life are things this type demands and gets. Whereas the Fleshy demands the comforts and the Flushed the unusual, the Muscular man demands the essentials. He is willing to work for them, so he usually succeeds.

He doesn't consider frills and luxuries as necessities, but demands the things everyday men or women need for everyday existence. Naturally he goes after them with the same force he displays in everything else.

His Heart and Soul in Things

When someone shows great intensity of action directed toward a definite end we often say "he puts his heart and soul into it." This phrase is fitting of almost everything the Muscular does. He makes no half-hearted attempts.

An Enthusiast

Emerson said: "Enthusiasm does all things". Thus, it makes sense why this type accomplishes so much. The reason behind the Muscular man's enthusiasm is interest.

Homo sapiens Alphabet

All emotions powerfully affect muscles. A sad thought darts through your mind and instantly the muscles of your face droop and the corners of your mouth go down. Hundreds of similar illustrations with which you are already familiar serve to prove how close the connection is between emotions and muscles. The heart itself is nothing more or less than a large, tough muscle.

Possessing the best equipment for expressing emotion, the Muscular is constantly and automatically using it. Therefore he becomes an enthusiast over many things during the course of his lifetime. This enthusiasm literally burns his way to the things he wants.

The Plain Talker

When deeply moved, this type talks well. If the mental element is also strong, he can become a good public speaker for he will then have all the qualifications—a powerful voice, human sympathy, enthusiasm, democracy, and simplicity.

In private conversation he is inclined to use the verbal hammers too much and to be too drastic in his statements, accusations, etc. But he means what he tells you, no more, and usually not much less.

He avoids long words and complicated phrases even when he is well-educated and speaks with directness and decisiveness.

Straightforward

"Straight from the hip" might be used to describe the method of the pure Muscular man in what he does and says. He does not deal in the fringe, dislikes the superfluous and the superficial. He goes through life over the shortest roads.

Homo sapiens Alphabet

Likes the Common People

Plain folks like him are the kind this type prefers for friends. He enjoys them immensely, but does not cultivate as large a number of them as does the Flushed, nor have as many acquaintances as the Fleshy type.

Snubs the Snobs

The snob is disliked by everyone, but he is specially loathed by this type. Being so democratic himself and living his life along such ordinary lines, he has no patience with people who imagine they are better than others or who carry the air of superiority.

The only person therefore the Muscular is inclined to snub is the snob. He is not overawed by him and enjoys "taking him down a peg or two," whenever he tries his high and mighty airs on him.

Defends the "Under Dog"

Standing by the underdog is a kind of religion with this type. He glories in fighting for the down trodden. This explains why he is so often a radical. Much of this vehemence in radicalism is due to the fact that he feels he is getting even with the snobs of the world—the plutocrats—when he furthers the causes of the proletariat.

Often on the Warpath

To "duke it out" with you is the first inclination of this type when he becomes angry. He is apt to say atrocious things and to exaggerate his grievances. Everything must yield to his "anger" once it is up.

Being possessed of highly developed fighting equipment, he is like a battleship, with every gun in place, most of the time.

He is frequently in violent quarrels with his friends, and since he does not recover from his anger quickly like the Flushed man, he often loses them for life.

The Most Generous Friend

When they like you the Muscular are the most abandoned in their generosity of all the types. They "go the limit" for you, as people say, and they go at it with their money, time, love and enthusiasm.

All types do this for short periods occasionally and for a very few choice friends. But the Muscular type often does it for people he scarcely knows if they strike his fancy or appeal to him.

His heart and his home belong to the stranger almost as completely as to his family, for he does not feel a stranger to anyone. He feels from the first moment, and acts, as though he had known you always.

This accounts for his democracy, for his success as an orator, and— sometimes for his being "broke."

Not a Quick Forgiver

But disappointing him in anything he considers vital and he does not overlook it easily. He finds it especially difficult to forgive people who take advantage of the generosity he so lavishly extends. But he does not make his hate a life-long one, as the Bony type does. With all his own giving to others he seldom takes much from others.

Homo sapiens Alphabet

The Naturally Independent

"Standing on his own legs" is a well-known trait of the Muscular. Dependence is bred of necessity. This type being able to get for him most of the things he wants, rarely finds it necessary to call upon others for assistance.

Love of self-government, plus fighting courage, both of which are inherent in the Muscular Irish race, are responsible for the long struggle for their independence.

Likes Plain Foods

"Meat and potatoes" are the favorite diet of the average American Muscular. The Fleshy type wants richness and sweetness in food, the Flushed type wants variety and delicacy, but the Muscular wants large quantities of plain food.

The Fleshy specializes in desserts, the Flushed in unusual dishes, but the Muscular wants solid fare. He is so fond of meat that it is practically impossible for him to confine himself to a vegetable diet.

When He is in Moderate Circumstances

The Muscular is most often found in moderate circumstances. He is rarely far below or far above them. Most of the plain, simple, everyday things he desires can be secured by people of average means. He does not feel the necessity for becoming a millionaire to obtain comforts like the Fleshy, or for extravagances like the Flushed type.

When He is Rich

Philanthropy marks the expenditures of this type whenever he is rich. He does not spend as much of his money for possessions but enjoys investing it in what he deems the real—that is, other human beings.

The most plain and durable things in furnishings, architecture, and service characterize the rich of this type in their homes.

The World's Work Done by the Muscular type

Broadly speaking, the Fleshy man manages the world, the Flushed man entertains the world, and the Muscular man does the work of the world.

He composes most of the day-laborers, the middle men, the manual and mechanical workers the world around, as we have stated before.

He could get out of his hard places into better paid ones if he did not like activity so well, but lacking the love of ease and appearance, he is willing to work hard for the necessities of life.

Simple Habits

The Muscular man's nature does not demand the exciting, the gregarious or the food-and-drink things that lead toward carelessness. He is seldom a spender. He likes to go to bed early, work hard and make practical progress in his life. He leads the simple and yet the most strenuous existence of any type.

Social Assets

His generosity is the strong social asset of the Muscular. He is usually straightforward and sincere and thereby gains the confidence of those who meet him.

Social Liabilities

His loud voice and his plain ways are sometimes the disadvantages. He needs polishing and is not inclined to take it. His forcefulness is also sometimes a severe drawback.

Emotional Assets

Understanding, enthusiasm and warmth of heart are the emotional qualities which help to make him the public leader he so often is. These have made him the "born orator," the radical and the reformer of all ages.

Emotional Liabilities

His tendency toward anger and combat are shackles that seriously handicap him. Many times, these lose him the big opportunities which his splendid traits might obtain for him.

Business Assets

Efficiency and willingness to work hard and long are the greatest business assets of this type.

Business Liabilities

Forcefulness over trivialities costs the average Muscular man many business chances. He has to fight out every issue and while he is doing it, the other fellow closes the deal. He is inclined to argue at great length. This helps him as a lawyer or speaker but it hurts him in business. Curbing his combativeness in business should be one of his foremost aims.

Strong Points

Democracy, industry, and great physical strength are the strong points of this type.

Weak Points

Inclination to overwork and to fight constitutes the Muscular man's two weak links.

How to Deal with this Type Socially

Don't put on airs or expect him to when you are meeting this type socially. Be straightforward and genuine with him if you would win him.

How to Deal with this Type in Business

Remember, this type is inclined to be efficient and democratic and you had better be the same if you wish to succeed with him in business. He is intensely resentful of the man who tries to put anything over on him and he demands efficiency. So when you promise him a thing, see to it that you deliver the goods and for the price stated. He does not mind paying a good price if he knows it in the beginning; but beware of raising it afterwards. The Muscular man is serious in business, not a jollier like the Fleshy, or a thriller like the Flushed type, and he wants you to be the same.

Remember, the chief distinguishing marks of the Muscular, in the order of their importance, are LARGE, FIRM MUSCLES, A SQUARE JAW and SQUARE HANDS. Any person who has these is largely of the Muscular type, no matter what other types may be included in his makeup.

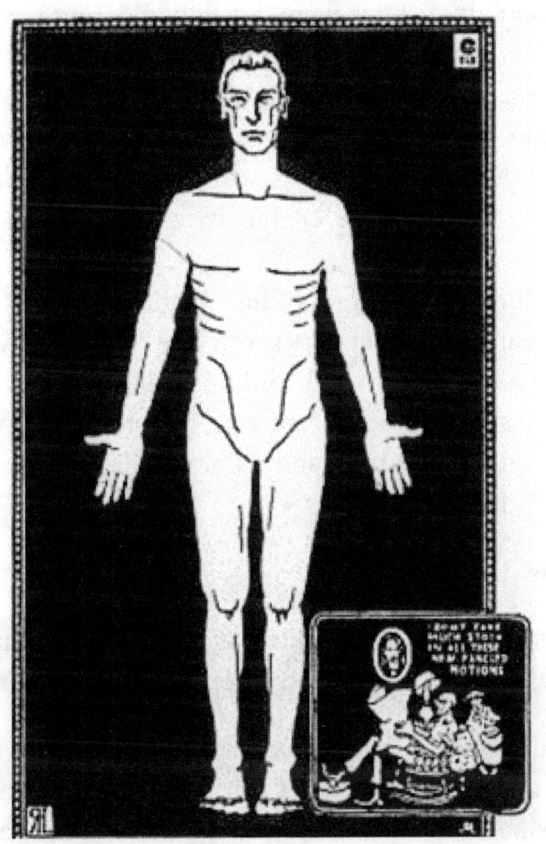

CHAPTER IV

THE BONY TYPE

"The Stayer"

Men and women in whom the Bony or bony framework of the body is more highly developed than any other system are called the Bony type. This system consists of the bones of the body and makes what we call the skeleton.

Homo sapiens Alphabet

Just as the previous systems were developed during man's biological evolution for purposes serving the needs of the organism—first, a stomach, then a transport system in the form of arteries to carry the food to remote parts of the body, and later muscles with which to move itself about—so this bony scaffolding was developed to hold the body upright and better enable it to defend and assert itself.

Man is a creature who, in spite of his height, walks erect. He can do so only by means of the support given him by his bony framework. The human body is like a tall building—the muscles are like the mortar and plaster, the bones are like the steel framework around which everything else is built and without which the structure could not stand upright.

How to Know Him

Prominent ankles, wrists, knuckles and elbows are sure signs that such an individual has a large bony element in his makeup.

When you look at any person you quickly discern whether flesh, bone, or muscle predominates in his construction. If flesh predominates he leans toward the Fleshy, no matter what other types he may have in combination; if firm, well-defined muscles are conspicuous, he is largely Muscular; but if his bones are *proportionately large for his body* he has much of the Bony type in his makeup.

The "Raw-Boned" Man

"Raw-boned" exactly describes the appearance of the extreme Bony man. Such a man is a contrast to others in any group and a figure with which all of us are familiar, but that his inner nature differs as widely from others as his external appearance differs from theirs.

As we proceed through this chapter you will be interested to note how every trait attributed to this type applies with uncanny accuracy to every extremely raw-boned, angular person you have ever known. You will also notice how these traits have predominated in every person whose bones were large for his body. Though this type was the last to be classified by science it is the most extreme of them all.

Physical Rigidity

An impression of physical rigidity is given by the extreme Bony type. Such a man or woman looks stable, unchanging, and immovable—as though he could take a stand and keep to it through thick and thin.

So vividly do very tall, angular, raw-boned people convey this impression that they are seldom approached by beggars or street peddlers.

His Size Looks Formidable

The power of his physique is evident to all who look at him. The strength indicated by his large joints, angular hands and general bulk intuitively warns others to let this kind of person alone.

He is therefore unmolested for the most part, whether he walks down the streets of his home town or wanders the streets of precarious neighborhood.

His Ruggedness

This type also looks rugged. He reminds us of "the rugged Rockies." He appears firm, fixed, and impassive—as though everything about him was permanent.

Externals are not accidental. They always correspond to the internal nature in every form of life. And it is not accidental that the Bony looks all of these things. He is all of them as definitely as they can be expressed in human nature.

The Steady Man

Of all human types the Bony is the most dependable and reliable. The phrases, "that man is steady," "never flies off the handle," "always the same," etc., are invariably used concerning those of more than average bony structure.

Immovability His Keynote

The keynote of the Bony man's whole nature—mental, physical and moral—is immovability.

Once he settles into a place of any kind—a town, a home, or even a chair—he is disinclined to move. He does not settle as quickly as other types but when he does it is for a longer stay.

Think how different he is from others in this psychological trait and how it coincides exactly with his physiological structure.

The Fleshy man lets you make temporary dents in his plans, but the Bony man is exactly the opposite, just as bone is difficult to twist, or turn, or alter in any way. It takes a long time and much effort—but once it is changed it is there for good.

Homo sapiens Alphabet

The "Six-Footer"

Because any individual's height is determined by his skeleton, extreme tallness is a sign of a larger than average bony structure. The extreme Bony type is therefore tall.

But you must remember that large joints are more significant than height. Even when found in short people they indicate a large Bony tendency.

Large Bones for His Body

So bear in mind that any person whose *bones are large for his body* is somewhat of the Bony type, regardless of whether he is short or tall and regardless of how much flesh or muscle he may have. The large-jointed person with presence of Fleshy traits is a Bony-Fleshy combination type. A large-jointed man of muscle would be a Bony-Muscular.

The "Small Bony"

A very short person then may be predominantly Bony if his bones are proportionately large for his body. Such an individual is called a "Small Bony."

A head that is high for his body and inclines to be straight up and down goes with the extreme Bony type. It does not resemble a sphere like the Fleshy, is not kite-shaped like the Flushed, or square like the Muscular type. It is higher than any of the others, stands on a longer, more angular neck, and his "Adam's Apple" is usually in evidence.

The Pioneer Type

Like each of the other types, the Bony traits are a result of a certain environment. Rigorous, remote regions require just such people, and these finally gave rise to this stoical nature. The outposts of civilization are responsible for his evolution.

Pioneering, with its hardship, its menacing cold and lack of comforts, in far countries at last produced a man who could stand them, who could "live through" almost anything and still dominate his surroundings.

Not a "Softie"

The Bony man does not give way to his feelings. He keeps his grief, sorrows, ambitions and most of his real opinions to himself. He is the farthest from a "softie" of any type.

If you desire to know at once what kind of person the Bony is, put the Fleshy and Flushed types together and mix them thoroughly. The Bony is the *opposite* of that mixture.

Each and every trait he possesses is one whose exact opposite you will find in one or the other of these first two types.

Consistency in Types

As we go on in this chapter you will see why all kinds of people make up the world, for Mother Nature has outdone herself in the distinctions between the five human types.

Each type is made up of certain groups of traits with which we have come in contact all our lives but which we have never classified and each "set" of traits comprising a type has a consistency which nothing less than Mother Nature could have produced. You will be interested to see how accurate the statements are concerning each type and how they are proven again and again in every type you associate with.

Guesswork is drastically reduced, if no longer necessary, in the sizing up of strangers. You can know them better than their mothers know them if you will get these nutshells of facts clearly in your mind and then *apply* them.

His High Cheek Bones

Cheek bones standing higher than the average are indicative either of a large Flushed or a large Bony element.

If the distance between the cheeks is so wide as to make this the widest section of the face, it is probable that the person is more a Flushed than a Bony. But if his face is narrow across the cheek bones, and especially if it runs perpendicularly down to the jaw-corners from that point instead of tapering, the person is large of the Bony type.

Built on the Oblong

An oblong is what the Bony brings to mind. His body outlines approximate the oblong—a squareness plus length. He is full of right angles and sharp corners.

His face is built on the oblong and if you will notice the side-head of the next Bony man you meet you will see that even a side view presents more nearly the appearance of the oblong than of any other geometrical figure.

The Oblong Hand

"The knotty hand" well describes that of the Bony. The hand outlines of this type also approximate the oblong. It runs straight down instead of tapering when the fingers are held close together. The hand of the Bony matches his body, head and face. It is bony, angular, large-jointed and as rigid as it looks. The inflexibility of his hand is always apparent in his handshake.

Knotty Fingers

Knotty fingers characterize the hands of this type. Their irregular appearance comes from the size of the joints which are large, in keeping with all the joints running throughout his organism.

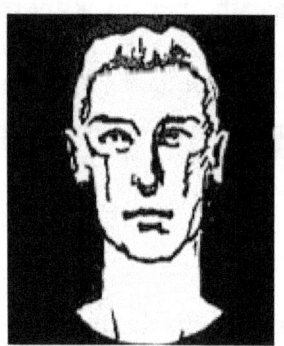 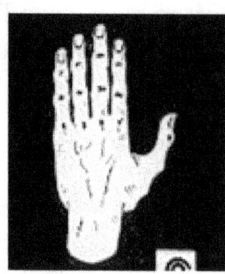

Typical Facial Features and Hand of the Bony Type

No Guesswork in Nature

Nature has no accidents. With her everything is organized, everything has a purpose, and every part of a thing, inside and out, matches the whole. So the hand of the Bony and the face of the Bony match the body and head.

This is also true of every other type. The Fleshy man has small, fleshy, dimpled hands and feet like his body; the Flushed has tapering hands and feet to match his face and body; the Muscular's body, hands and feet are all square; but the Bony man has a bony body, so his hands and feet are equally bony.

The Man of Slow Movements

"He is too slow for me," you have heard someone say of another. Perhaps you heard it said today. Review the outward appearance of all the people you know who have this reputation, from those of your earliest childhood down to that person of whom it was spoken today—and you will find that every one of them resembled the Bony type we have just been describing.

Look back and call to mind the appearance of all the "quick" ones and you will find that in every case they possessed high color, high chests or high-bridged noses. Take another look for the easy-going affable ones, and see how plump they all were!

The Straight-Laced

None of these things "just happened." They are the result of the law of cause and effect. The connection between external and internal traits is becoming clearer every day and reveals some very unexpected things.

One that has been discovered very recently is that the straight-faced are the straight-laced. Notice for yourself and you will find that every person who is really "straight-laced" is a person with a straight face—that is, a face with straighter up-and-down lines than the average.

Think back over those you have known who come under this heading and you will find no actually round-faced people amongst them.

No matter how sanctimonious, religious, or proper a person may act when his position or the occasion demands it, if he has a round, "moon" face he is not really straight-laced at heart. Anyone who knows him well enough to know his real nature will tell you so.

The Naturally Conventional

The "born Puritan," the ascetic, and the naturally conventional person is, on the other hand, invariably an individual of more severe facial outlines.

This person may be in an unconventional position; your straight-faced, severe-lined person may be a gambler, a bootlegger, or follow any other route defying the conventions; but he is at heart a conservative after all. For instance, you will always find, when you know him, that he does things in a way that is very conventional to him. That is, he has decided standards, rules, habits and requirements, and he clings rigidly to them in the transaction of his business, regardless of how laidback the business itself may be.

"A certain way of doing things" means as much to him, at heart, as it means little to the circular-faced people.

Systematic and Methodical

Homo sapiens Alphabet

"A place for everything and everything in its place" is a rule preached and practiced by people of this type.

The Bony person does not misplace his things. He knows so well where they are that he can "go straight to them in the dark." Such a man is careful of his tools and keeps his work-bench or desk "spick-and-span." A woman of this type is an excellent housekeeper. Her sewing basket, dresser drawers and pantry shelves are all systematically arranged in order.

The typical New England housewife, who washes on Mondays, irons on Tuesdays and bakes on Saturdays for forty years, is a direct descendant of the Puritans, most of whom belong to this bony, pioneering type.

The Stiff Sitter

Extremely Bony people are inclined to be somewhat formal in their movements. They make fewer motions than any other type. They do not wave their hands or arms about when talking and are almost devoid of gesticulation of any kind. They sit upright instead of slumping down in their chairs.

The Bony Walk

The extremely raw-boned person has also a formal gait. His walk, like all his other movements, is inclined to be deliberate and somewhat mechanical. Nothing about the five types is more interesting than the walk which distinguishes each. The Fleshy undulates or rolls along; the Flushed is an impulsive walker, and the Muscular is forceful in his walk. But the Bony walks mechanically, deliberately, and refuses to hurry or speed up.

Homo sapiens Alphabet

The Naturally Poised

The Bony man has more natural poise than any other type. He is not impressionable, excitable or arousable. Things do not "stir him up" as they do other people. He is more self-contained, self-controlled and self-sufficient than any other. He is not easily carried off his feet and seldom yields to impulse. It is difficult to get him to do anything on the spur of the moment. He usually has his evenings, Sundays and vacations all planned in advance and won't change his schedule.

Not Given to "Nerves"

Literally as well as figuratively the Bony is not a man of "nerves." Every fiber of his being is less susceptible to outside stimuli than that of other types. In this he is the exact opposite of the Flushed whose nerves, as we have pointed out, are so finely organized that he is hypersensitive.

Resists Change

Bony people do not change anything, from their hair style to their minds, any more frequently than necessary. When they do, it is for what they consider overpoweringly good reasons.

These people are not flighty. They have their work, their time and their lives laid out systematically and do not allow trivialities to upset them. They take a longer time to deliberate on a proposed plan of action, but once they have made a decision, adhere to it with much greater tenacity than any other type.

The Constant

People of this type are not fickle or flirtatious. They love few; but once having become enamored, they are not easily turned aside. It is this type that remains true to one love through many years, sometimes for life.

The Implacable

The Bony are not prone to sudden outbursts of temper. But they have the unbending kind when it is aroused. Never forgiving and never forgetting are traits of these people as contrasted with the Flushed type.

The Fleshy avoids those he does not like and forgets them because it is too much bother to hate; the Flushed flames up one moment and forgives the next; the Muscular takes it out in a fight then and there, or argues with you about it.

But the Bony despises, hates and loathes—and keeps on for years after every one else has forgotten all about it. The "rock-bound Puritan" type, as stony as the New England land from which it gets its living, is always Bony. The implacable father who turns his child away from home, with orders "never to show up at his door again," always has a lot of bone in his structure. Those who refuse to be softened into forgiveness by the years are always of this type.

Not Adaptable

It is difficult for the Bony to "fit in." He is not adaptable and in this is once again the opposite of the Flushed. It is impossible for him to adjust himself quickly to people or places. Because he is unyielding, unbending and unadjustable he is called "set in his ways."

Homo sapiens Alphabet

He should not be misjudged for this inadaptability; however, it is as natural to him as smoothness is to the Fleshy and impulsiveness to the Flushed type. He is made that way and is no more to blame for it than you are for having brown eyes instead of blue.

The One-Track Man

"Single-track mind" is characteristic of this type. They get an idea or an attitude and it is there to stay. They think the same things for many years and follow a few definite lines of action most of their lives.

But it is to be remembered in this connection that this type often accomplishes more through his intensive concentration than more versatile types. While they follow many by-paths in search of their goal the Bony sticks to the main track.

The Born Specialist

"This one thing I do," is a motto of the Bony. They are the least versatile of any type and do not like to jump from one kind of work to another. They prefer to do one thing at a time, do it well and finish it before starting anything else. Because of this, the Bony are specialists.

An old friend of mine, Justin, was this type. He and I started learning about Cisco Networking (CCNA) years ago. He kept at it and now becomes a specialist in computer networking while I changed to sales.

Dislikes Many Irons in the Fire

The man who likes many irons in the fire is never a Bony. To have more than one problem before him at one time makes him irritable, upset and exasperated.

The Most Dependable Type

The unchangingness which handicaps the Bony man in so many ways is responsible for one very admirable trait. That trait is dependability. The Bony man is reliable. He can be taken at his word more often than any other type because he lives up to it with greater care.

Always on Time

When a Bony person says, "I will meet you at four o'clock at the corner of Main and Market," he will arrive at Main and Market at *four* o'clock. He will not come straggling along, or plead interruptions, nor give excuses. He will be on the exact spot at the exact hour.

In this, he is again a contrast to the first two types. A Fleshy man will roll into the meeting at a quarter after four, or more likely, a half hour past the time, smilingly apologize and be so naive you forgive and let it go at that.

The Flushed person will arrive anywhere from five after four to six o'clock, drown you in a thrilling narrative of just how it all happened, and never give you a chance to voice your anger till he has smoothed it all out of you.

An Exacting Man

But the Bony is disdainful of such tactics and you had better beware of using them on him. He is dependable himself and demands it of others—a little trait all of us have regarding our own particular virtues.

Likes Responsibility

Responsibility, if it does not entail too many different kinds of thought and work, is enjoyed by the Bony type.

He can be given a task, a job, a position and he will attend to it. Entrust him with a commission of any kind, from getting you a certain kind of thread to discovering the North Pole, and he will come pretty near carrying it out, if he undertakes it.

Finishes What He Starts

If a Bony man decides to do a piece of work for you, you can go ahead and forget all about it. No need to advise, urge, watch, inspire, coax and cajole him to keep him at it. He prefers to keep at a thing if he starts it himself. You may have to hurry him but you will not have to watch him in order to know he is sticking to his task. This type starts few things but he brings those few to a pretty successful conclusion.

Takes the Opposite Side

"If you want him to do a thing, tell him to do the opposite," is a well-known rule supposed to work with certain kinds of people.

You have wondered why it sometimes worked and sometimes didn't, but it is no mystery to the student of Human Analysis.

When it worked, the person you tried it on was a Bony or one largely bony in type. When it didn't, he was of some other type.

"Contrary?" complained a man of a bony neighbor, "Contrary is his middle name."

"I am open to conviction but I would like to see the man who could convince me!" is always said by a man whose type you will be sure to recognize.

An "Againster"

"I don't know what it is but I'm against it," is the inside mental attitude of the extremely raw-boned, angular man or woman.

They often, unconsciously, refrain from making a decision about a thing till the other fellow makes his. That settles it; they take the other side.

Think back over your school-days and call to mind the visage and bodily shape of the boy who was always on the opposite side, who just naturally disagreed, who "stood out" against the others. He was a bony lad every time.

Remember the "Fleshy" with a face like a full moon? Did he do such things? He did not. He was amenable, easy-going, good natured, and didn't care how the discussion came out, as long as it didn't delay the lunch hour.

Remember the boy or girl who had the pick of the school for company whenever there was a party, who danced well and was so sparkling that you always felt like a pebble competing against a diamond when they were around? That boy or girl had a high chest, or high color, or a high-bridged nose—and usually all three.

But the one you couldn't persuade, who couldn't be won over, who refused to give in, who held up all the unanimous votes till everybody was disgusted with him, and who rather gloried in the distinction—that boy had big bones and a square jaw—the proof that he was a combination of the Bony and Muscular types.

Wears Same Style Ten Years

Even the clothes worn by this type tell the same story. Styles may come and styles may go, but the Bony goes on forever wearing the same lines and the same general fashions he wore ten years before. Bony people find a kind of clothes that just suit, and to those clothes they will stick for twenty years!

Disdains the Fashions

In every city, neighborhood and country crossroads there is always somebody who defies the styles of today by wearing the styles of ten years ago. Every such person is sure a bony individual. In every case you will find that his face is longer, his nose is longer, or his jaw and hands are longer than the average—all Bony indications.

When He is Rich

The Bony man's adherence to one style or to one clothes is not primarily because he wishes to save money, though saving money is an item that he never overlooks. It is due rather to his inability to change anything about himself in accordance with outside influence until a long time has elapsed.

Doesn't Spend Money Lavishly

The Bony is, as stated at the head of this chapter, a "stayer" and this applies to everything he wears, thinks, says, believes, and to the way he carries on every activity of his life. No matter how rich he may be he will not buy one kind of car today and another tomorrow, or one house this week and another in six weeks.

He uses his money, as all of us do, to maintain his type-habits and to give freer rein to them, not to change them to any extent. This type likes sameness. He likes to "get acquainted" with a thing. He never takes up fads and is the most conservative of all types. Unlike the Flushed, he avoids extremes in everything and dislikes anything savoring of the "showy" or conspicuous.

Not a Social Star

Because he dislikes display, refuses to yield to the new chic fashions of polite society and finds it hard to adapt himself to people, the man of this type is seldom a social success.

He is the least of a "ladies' man" of all the types. The Bony woman is even less disposed to social life than the Bony man because the business and professional demands, which compel men of this type to mingle with their fellows, are less urgent with her.

Likes the Same Food

The same "yesterday, today and forever" is the kind of food preferred by this type. He seldom orders anything new. The tried and true things he has eaten for twenty-five years are his favorites and it is almost impossible to win him away from them. "I have had bread and milk for supper every Sunday night for thirty years," a Bony man said to us not long ago.

Means What He Says

The Bony does not flatter and seldom praises. Even when he would like to, the words do not come easily. But when he does give you a compliment you may know he means it. He is incisive and specific—a little too much so to grace modern social intercourse where so much is froth.

A Man of Few Words

A man of few words is always and invariably a man whose bones are large for his body. The fleshy man uses up a great many pleasant, suave, merry, harmless words; the Flushed inundates you with conversation; the Muscular argues, declares and states; but the Bony alone is sparing of his words.

The Hoarder

Bony people are never lavish with anything. They do not waste anything nor throw anything away. These are the people who save things and store them away for years against the day when they may find some use for them. When they do part with them it is always to pass them on "where they will do someone some good."

Careful of Money

You never saw a stingy Fleshy man in your life. Imagine a two-hundred-pound miser! Neither have you ever seen a really stingy man who was red-faced and high-chested. Nor have you ever found a real Muscular who was a "tightwad."

But you have known some people who were pretty close with their money. And every one of them was inclined to boniness.

When He is Poor

Bony men are seldom "broke" for they are more careful of expenditures than any other type. Even when they receive small salaries this type of person always has something laid by. But the extreme Bony seldom makes a million. The same caution which prevents his spending much money also prevents the plunges that make big money.

The Bony cares more for money than anyone else. This is what has enabled him, when combined with some other type, to be so successful in banking—a business where you risk the other man's money, not your own.

The extreme Bony type is never careless or extravagant with his money no matter how much he has. He never believes in paying any more for a thing than is necessary. Take note of the men who carry purses for coins instead of letting their change lie loose in their pockets. They are bony every time! Fleshy and Flushed people are the ones who let their greenbacks fall on the floor while paying the cashier!

Fear of the Future

"The rainy day" doesn't worry the Fleshy or the Flushed ones, but it is seldom out of the consciousness of the Bony men and women. So they cling to their two-hundred-and-fifty-dollar-a-week menial jobs for years because they are afraid to tackle anything entailing risk.

Pays His Bills

"I had rather trust a Bony man than any other kind," is what the credit experts said. "Other things being equal, he is the most reliable type in money matters, and pays his bills more promptly."

The Bony man is one who seldom approaches the credit man, however. He usually has enough to get the few things he really wants and if not he waits till he has.

Extreme Bony husbands give their wives smaller allowances in proportion to their total income than any other type, and because they are systematic themselves they are more likely to ask for reports and itemizations as to where it goes.

The Fleshy husbands and the Flushed husbands are the ones who give their wives their last cent and never ask what becomes of it.

The Repressed Man

The Bony man or woman is always somewhat repressed. Unlike the Flushed, who uncorks and bubbles like a champagne bottle, he keeps the lid on his feelings.

Bony people are always more reticent than others. They invariably tell less of their private or personal affairs. One may live across the hall from a Bony man for years without knowing much about him. He is secretive and guarded.

Loyal to His Few Friends

"Once your friend always your friend" can be said about the Bony oftener than any other type. The Bony does not make friends easily and is not a "mixer" but keeps his friends for many years. He "takes to" very few people but is exceedingly loyal to those of his choice.

The "BedRock"

People of the Bony type say little, they do little for you and they do not gush—but they are always there when you need them and "always the same." They write few letters to you when away, and use few words and little paper when they do. They are likely to fill every page, to write neatly, to waste no margins and to avoid embellishments. Their letters seldom require an extra stamp.

Plans Ahead

Foresight, laying plans far into the future, and keeping an eye out for breakers ahead, financially and otherwise, are tendencies which come natural to the Bony. He does not like to wait until the last moment to do a thing. He dislikes unexpectedness and emergencies of any kind. He is always prepared. For instance a Bony person will think out every move of a long journey before boarding his plane or train. Weeks in advance he will have the schedule marked and put away in his coat pocket—and he knows just which coat he is going to wear too!

People He Dislikes

The Bony man does not like people who try to speed him up, hurry him, or make him change his habits. Flashy people irritate him. But his worst repulsion is when people try to dictate to him. This type cannot be driven. The only way to handle him is to let him think he is having his own way.

Likes the Submissive

Amenable people who never interfere with him yet lend themselves to his plans, desires and eccentricities are the favorites of this type.

Social Assets

The Bony has no traits which can properly be called social assets. His general uprightness comes nearest to standing him in good stead socially, however.

Social Liabilities

Stiffness, reticence, physical awkwardness and the inability to present or to praise are the chief social handicaps of this type.

Emotional Assets

The Bony is not emotional and cannot be said to possess any assets that are purely emotional.

Emotional Liabilities

The lack of emotional fervor and enthusiasm prevents this type from impressing others.

Business Assets

Keeping his word, orderliness and system are the primary business assets of this type.

Business Liabilities

The reluctance to mix, the inability to adapt himself to his patrons, and the tendency to be too rigid with people are the business handicaps of the Bony.

His Strong Points

Dependability, honesty, economy, faithfulness and his capacity for finishing what he starts are the strong points of this type.

His Weak Points

Stubbornness, obstinacy, slowness, over-cautiousness, coldness and a tendency to stinginess are the weak links in people of the extreme Bony type.

I had a friend who belongs to this Bony type many years ago. I borrowed 2 dollars from him to buy a hotdog and forgot about the debt. He made a point to borrow exactly 2 dollars from me. As soon as I gave him the 2 dollars, he said to me: "Now we are even."

How to Deal with this Type Socially

There is little to be done with the Bony when you meet him socially except to let him do what he wants to do. Don't interfere with him if you want him to like you.

How to Deal with this Type in Business

As an employee, give him responsibility and then let him alone to do it his way. Then keep your hands off. Don't give him constant advice; don't try to drive him. Let him be as systematic as he likes. When dealing with him in business, rely on him and let him know you admire his dependability.

Remember, the distinguishing marks of the Bony, in the order of their importance, are PROPORTION ATELY LARGE BONES FOR THE BODY, PROMINENT JOINTS and A LONG FACE. Any person who has these is largely of the Bony type no matter what other types may be included in his makeup.

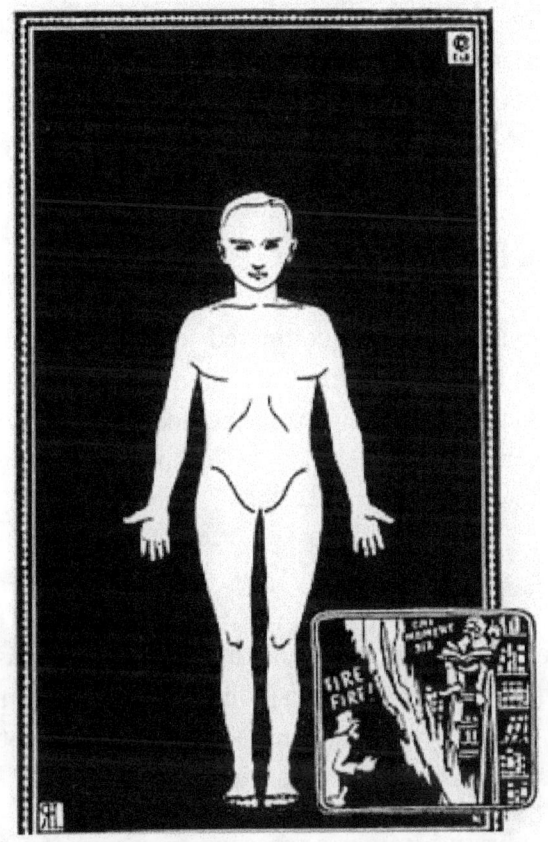

CHAPTER V

THE BRAINY TYPE

"The Thinker"

All those in whom the nervous system is more highly developed than any other are the Brainy type. This system consists of the brain and nerves.

Meditation, imagination, dreaming, visualizing and all voluntary mental processes take place in the cerebrum, or brain, as we shall call it. The brain is the headquarters of the nervous system—its "home office"—just as the stomach is the home office of the Fleshy type and the heart and lungs the home office of the Flushed.

Your Transport System

The Flushed system may be compared to a great transport system, with each of its tributaries—from the main trunk arteries down to the tiniest blood vessels—starting from the heart and carrying its cargo of blood to every part of the body by means of the power furnished by the pumping of the heart.

Your Mother Board

But the nervous system is more like a Mother Board. Its network of nerves runs from every outlying point of the body into the great headquarters of the brain, carrying sense messages notifying us of everything heard, seen, touched, tasted or smelled.

As soon as the brain receives a message from any of the five senses it decides what to do about it and if action is decided on, sends its orders back over the nerve wires to the muscles telling them what action to perform.

Your Working Agents

This latter fact—that the muscles are the working agents of the body—also explains why the Muscular type is naturally more active than any of the others.

Homo sapiens Alphabet

Source of Your Raw Materials

The body may be compared to a perfectly organized transportation system and factory combined. The Fleshy system furnishes the raw materials for all the systems to work on.

Stationary Equipment

The bones of the body are like the telephone poles, the bridges and structures for the protection and permanence of the work carried on by the other systems of the body.

Now poles, bridges and structures are less movable, less alterable than any of the other parts of a transportation system, and likewise the bony element in man makes him less alterable in every other way than he would otherwise be. A predominance of it in any individual indicates a dominance of this immovable tendency in his nature.

Mind and matter are so inseparably bound up together in man's organism that it is impossible to say just where mind ends and matter begins. But this we know: that even the mind of the Bony person partakes of the same unbending qualities that are found in the bones of his body.

"Every Cell Thinks"

Thomas A. Edison, as level-headed a scientist as ever lives, says, "Every cell in us thinks." Human Analysis proves to us that something very near this is the case for it shows how the habitual mental processes of every individual are always "off the same piece of goods" as his body.

Homo sapiens Alphabet

Thus the Fleshy man's mind acts as his body acts—evenly, unhurriedly, easefully and comfortably. The Flushed man's mind has the same quickness and resourcefulness that distinguish all his bodily processes. The Muscular man's mind acts in the same strenuous way that his body acts, while the Bony man's brain always has an immovable quality closely akin to the boniness of his body.

The Large Head on the Small Body

As pointed out before, the larger any organ or system the more will it tend to express itself. So, the large-headed, small-bodied man runs more to mental than to physical activities, and is invariably more mature in his thinking. Conversely, the Fleshy type gets his traits from that elemental stage in human development when we did little but get and absorb food, and when thinking was of the simplest form. In those days man was more physical than mental; he had a large stomach but a small head.

So today we see in the pure Fleshy type people who resemble their Fleshy ancestors. They have the same proportionately large stomach and proportionately small head,—with the stomach-system dominating their thoughts, actions and lives.

The Brainy is the exact opposite of this. He has a top-heavy head, proportionately large for his body, and a proportionately undeveloped stomach system.

His Small Fleshy System

The extreme Brainy differs from other types chiefly in the fact that while his head is unusually large compared to the body, his digestive, cardiopulmonary, muscular, and skeletal systems are smaller and less developed than the average. The latter fact is due to the same law which causes the Fleshy man to have a large body and a small head. Nature is a wonderful efficiency engineer. She provides only as much space as is required for the functioning of any particular organ, giving extra space only to those departments that need it.

The Brainy-Fleshy is the combination which makes most of the "magnates" and the self-made millionaires. Such a man has all the Fleshy type's desires for the luxurious comforts and "good things of life," combined with sufficient brains to enable him to make the money necessary to get them.

Nature doesn't give the pure Fleshy a large skull because he doesn't need it for the housing of his proportionately small brain, but concentrates on giving him a big stomach fitted with "all modern conveniences." On the other hand, the head of the Brainy is large because his brain is large. The skull which is pliable and unfinished at birth grows to conform to the size and shape of the brain as the glove takes on the shape of the hand inside it.

Stomach vs. Brain

Because the Fleshy and Brainy systems are farthest removed from each other, evolutionarily, a large brain and a large stomach are a very unusual combination. Such an individual would be a combination of the Fleshy and Brainy types and would have the Fleshy's plump body with a large highbrow head of the Brainy. The possession of these two highly developed but opposite kinds of systems places their owner constantly in the predicament of deciding between the big meal he wants and the small one he knows he should have for good brain work.

We are constructed that brain and stomach—each of which demands an extra supply of blood when performing its work—cannot function with maximum efficiency simultaneously.

Why Light Lunches

When your stomach is busy digesting a big meal your brain takes a vacation. This little fact is responsible for millions of light luncheons daily. The strenuous manual worker can empty a full dinner pail and profit by it but the brain worker long ago discovered that a heavy midday meal gave him a heavy brain for hours afterwards.

Clear Thinking and a Clear Stomach

Clear thinking demands a clear stomach because an empty stomach means that the blood, reserved necessary to vivid thinking, are free to go to the brain. Without good blood coursing at a fairly rapid rate through the brain man cannot think keenly or concentratedly. This explains why you think of so many important things when your stomach is empty that never occur to you when your energy is being monopolized by digestion.

Heavy Dinners and Heavy Speeches

Public speakers have learned that a heavy dinner means a heavy speech. They avoid eating a heavy dinner before making a speech.

Uses His Head

Homo sapiens Alphabet

Just as digestion is the favorite activity of the Fleshy type, head work is the favorite activity of the large-headed Brainy. He is so far removed, evolutionarily, from the stomach stage that his stomach is as much a remnant with him as the brain is a rudiment with the extreme Fleshy. The extra blood supply which nature furnishes to any over-developed part of the body also tends to encourage him in thinking, just as the same condition encourages the Fleshy man in eating.

Forgets to Eat

A Fleshy person never forgets dinner time. But the Brainy is so much more interested in food for his brain than food for his body that he can go without his meals and not mind it. He is likely to have a book and a cracker at his meals—and then forget to eat the cracker!

Physical Sensitivity

We are "mental" in proportion to the sensitiveness of our mental organization. The Brainy person possesses the most highly developed brain center of any type and is therefore more sensitive to all those stimuli which act upon the mind.

His whole body indicates it. The fineness of his features is in direct contrast to some of the other types. The unusual size of his brain denotes a correspondingly intricate organization of nerves, for the nerves are tiny elongations of the brain.

The intellectual sensitivity of any individual can be accurately estimated by noting the comparative size of his brain and body.

His Triangular Head and Face

A triangle is the geometrical figure approximated by the Brainy man's face and head. If he is a pure, extreme Brainy a triangle is again what you are reminded of when you look at his head from the side, for his head stands on a small neck, his forehead stands out at the top, while back of his head is long. These bring the widest part of his head nearer the top than we find it in other types.

Delicate Hands

A thin, delicate hand denotes a larger-than-average Brainy element.

Smooth Fingers

What have long been known as "smooth fingers" are typical of the Brainy type. These are not to be confused with the fleshy, pudgy babyish fingers of the Fleshy type. The Fleshy person's fingers are smooth and round; they do not present straight outlines at the sides. They puff out between the joints.

Smooth fingers are characteristic of the extreme Brainy type. They are called this because their outlines run straight up and down.

The joints of the Fleshy finger mark the narrowest places owing to the fact that the joints are not changeable. In the Bony fingers the opposite is true. The joints mark the widest spots and the spaces between   are   sunken.

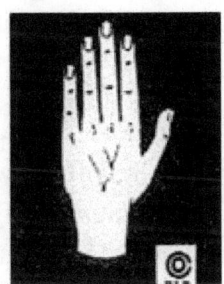

Typical Facial Features and Hand of the Brainy Type

The fingers of the Flushed are inclined to be pointed like his head, while the Muscular man's fingers are square at the end and look the power they possess.

But the Brainy has fingers unlike any of these. There is no flesh to make them pudgy and no muscle to make them firm. Neither are there large joints to make them knotty. Their outlines therefore run in almost straight lines and the whole hand presents a more delicate, aesthetic appearance.

Meditation His Keynote

Thinking, contemplating, reflecting—all the mental processes coming under the head of "meditation"—constitute the keynote of this type.

The Fleshy man lives to eat, the Flushed to feel, the Muscular to act, the Bony to stabilize, but the Brainy lives to meditate.

Air Castles

Homo sapiens Alphabet

He loves to plan, imagine, day-dream, visualize and go over and over in his mind the multiple possibilities, probabilities and potentialities of many things.

When he carries this to extremes—as the person with a huge head and tiny body is likely to do—he often overlooks the question of the practicability of the thing he is planning. He inclines to go "off on a tangent," to dream dreams that are near impossible of realization.

Thought for Thought's Sake

He will sit by the hour or by the day thinking out endless ultimate, for the sheer pleasure it gives him. Other men blame him, criticize him and ridicule him for this and for the most part he does fail of the practical success by which the efficient American measures everything.

But the fact must never be forgotten that the world owes its progress to the men who could see beyond their nose, who could conceive of things no one had ever actually seen. This type, more than any other, has been the innovator in all forms of human progress.

The Dreamer

"Everything accomplished starts with the dream," is a saying we all know to be true. Yet we go on forever giving all the big prizes to the doers. But the man, who can only dream, lives in a very hostile world. His real world is his thoughts but whenever he steps out of them into human society he feels like a stranger and he is one.

Doesn't Fit

Homo sapiens Alphabet

The world of today is ruled by people who accomplish. "Delivering the goods," "Delivering World Class services," are a part of our language because they represent the standards of the average American today.

The Brainy man is as much out of place in such an environment as a fish is on dry land. He knows it and he shows it. He doesn't know what the other kind are driving at and they know so little of what he is driving at that they have invented a special name for him—the "Mad Scientist."

Doing isn't his line. He prefers the pleasures of "thinking over". This success rate for this type is not high because he takes it all out in dreaming without ever doing the things necessary to make his dream come true.

A "Visionary"

These penchants for overlooking the obvious, the tangible and the necessary elements in everyday existence tend to make the Brainy what he is so often called—a "visionary."

For instance, he will build up in his mind the most imposing superstructure for an invention and confidently tell you "it will make millions," but forget to inform himself on such essential questions as "will it work?" "Is it transportable?" or "Is there any demand for it?"

Ahead of His Time

"He was born ahead of his time" applies most often to a man of this type. He has brains to see what the world needs and, not infrequently, sees how the world could get it. But he is so averse to action himself that unless active people take up his schemes, they seldom materialize.

What We Owe to the Dreamers

Men in whom the Brainy type is predominated anticipate every step man has made in his political, social, individual, industrial, religious and economic evolution. They have seen it decades and sometimes centuries in advance. But they were always ridiculed at first.

The Mutterings of Morse

History is full of stories of unappreciated genius. In Washington, D. C., you will have pointed out to you a great elm, made historic by Samuel Morse, inventor of the telegraph. He could not make the successful people of his day listen to him and invest in his idea, but he was so wrapped up in his invention that he used to sit under this tree whenever the weather permitted, and explain all about it to the down-and-outers and anyone else who would stop. "Listen to the mutterings of that poor old fool" said the "wise" men as they hurried by on the other side of the street. But today people come from everywhere to see "The Famous Morse Elm" and pay homage to the great mind that invented the telegraph.

"Langley's Folly"

Today we fly from continent to continent and air travel is superseding land and water transportation whenever great speed is in demand. A man receives word that his child is dangerously ill; he steps into an airplane and in less than a fraction of the time it would take trains or motors to carry him, descends at his own door.

Commerce, industry, war and the future of whole nations are being revolutionized by this man-made miracle. However, S. P. Langley was sneered at from one end of this country to the other because he was working on inventing a mechanical flying machine

The Trivial Telephone

Alexander Graham Bell invented the telephone. But it was many years before he could induce anybody to finance it, though some of the wealthiest, and therefore supposedly wisest, business men of the day were asked to do so. None of them would risk a dollar on it. Even after it had been tested at the Centennial Exposition in Philadelphia and found to work perfectly, its possibilities were so little realized that for a long while no one could be found to furnish the funds necessary to place it upon the market.

The Wizardry of Wireless

Then after the world had become accustomed to transacting millions of dollars' worth of business daily over the once despised telegraph and telephone it took out its doubts on Marconi and his "wireless telegraphy." "It's impossible," they said. "Talk without wires? Never!"

An Ideal Combination

The ideal combination is a dreamer who can DO or a doer who knows the power of a DREAM. Thinking and acting—almost every individual is doing too much of one and too little of the other!

To be a Success

Homo sapiens Alphabet

To be a successful individual today you have got to DREAM and then DO; plan and then PRODUCE; contemplate and then CONSTRUCT; think it out and then WORK it out.

If you do the latter at the expense of the former you are doomed to work forever for other people, to play some other man's game. If you do the former at the expense of the latter you are doomed to know only the fringes of life, never to be taken seriously and never to achieve.

Pitfalls for Dreamers

If you are inclined to take your pleasure in cogitating instead of creating; if it suffices you to see a thing in your imagination whether it ever comes to pass or not, you are at a decided disadvantage in this hustling world; and you will never make them a reality.

Pitfalls for the Doer

On the other hand if you are content to do what other men dream about and never have dreams of your own you will probably always have a job but will never have a million dollars. You will exist but you will never know what it is to live.

The Hungry Philosopher

The extreme Brainy man can sit on a park bench with an empty purse and an empty stomach and get as much pleasure out of reflecting on the philosophical questions of the world as a Fleshy man gets out of a juicy steak. Needless to say, each is an enigma to the other. Yet most people imagine that because both are human and both walk on their hind legs they are alike. They are no more alike than a cow and a canary.

His Frail Body

The extreme Brainy type finds it difficult to do things because, as we have seen, he is deficient in muscle—one of the vital elements upon which activity and accomplishment are based. This type has little muscle, little bone, and little flesh.

Deficient in "Horse Power"

He is not inactive for the same reason that the Fleshy is; his stomach processes do not slow him down. But his muscles are so under-developed that he has little inward urge toward activity and little force back of his movements. His heart and lungs are small, so that he also lacks "steam" and "horse power."

He prefers to sit rather than to move, exactly as the Muscular prefers to be "up and doing" rather than to sit still.

The Man of Futile Movements

Did you ever look on while a pure Brainy man tried to move a kitchen stove? Ever ask the dreamer in your house to bring down a trunk from the attic?

Will you ever forget the almost human perversity with which that stove and that trunk resisted him; or how amusing it looked to see a grown man outwitted at every turn by an inert mass?

His Jerky Walk

Because he is short, the Brainy man takes short steps. Because he lacks muscle, he lacks a powerful stride. As a result he has a walk that is irregular and sometimes jerky. When he walks slowly this jerk is not apparent; but when hurried, it is quite noticeable.

Is Lost in Chairs

The Brainy gets lost in the same chair that is itself lost under the large, spreading Bony and for the same reason. Built for the average, chairs are as much too large for the Brainy as they are too small for the big Bony man. So the Brainy man's legs dangle and his arms don't reach.

Dislikes Social Life

Though a most sympathetic friend, the Brainy does not make many friends and does not care for many. He is too abstract to add to the vivacity of social gatherings, for these are based on the enjoyment of the concrete.

Enjoys the Intellectuals

Readers, thinkers, writers—intellectuals like himself—are the kinds of people the Brainy enjoys most. Another reason why he has few friends is because these people, being in the great minority, are not easy to find.

Ignores the Ignorant

People who let others do their thinking for them and those who are not aware of the great things going on in world movements, are not popular with this type. He sometimes has a secret contempt for them and ignores them as completely as they ignore him.

Homo sapiens Alphabet

Avoids the Limelight

Modesty and reserve, almost as marked in the men as in the women, characterize this extreme type. They do things of great moment sometimes—invent something or write something extraordinary—but even then they try to avoid being glorified.

They prefer the shadows rather than the spotlight. Thus they miss many of the good things less brainy and more aggressive people gain. But it does no good to explain this to a Brainy man. He enjoys retirement and is constantly missing opportunities because he refuses to "mix."

Cares Little for Money

Friends mean something to the Brainy, fame sometimes means much but money means little. In this he is the exact opposite of the Bony, to whom the economic advantages or disadvantages of a thing are always significant.

The pure Brainy man finds it difficult to interest himself in his finances. He seldom counts his change. He will go away from his room leaving every cent he owns lying on the dresser—and then forget to lock the door!

This type of person almost never asks for a raise. He is too busy dreaming dreams to plan what he will do in his old age. He prefers staying at the same job with congenial associates to finding another even if it paid more.

Very Often Poor

Homo sapiens Alphabet

Since we get only what we go after in this world, it follows that the Brainy type is often poor. To make money one must want money. Competition for it is so keen that only those who want it badly and work with efficiency ever get very much of it.

The Brainy takes so little interest in money that he gets lost in the shuffle. Not until he wakes up some morning with the poorhouse staring him in the face does he give it serious consideration. And then he does not do much about it.

Almost Never Rich

History shows that few people of the pure Brainy type ever became rich. Even the most brilliant gave so much more thought to their mission than the practical ways and means that they were usually seriously handicapped for the funds necessary to its materialization.

About Clothes

Clothes are almost the last thing the Brainy thinks about. As we have seen, all the other types have decided preferences as to their clothes—the Fleshy man demands comfort, the Flushed style, the Muscular durability and the Bony sameness—but the extreme Brainy type says "anything will do." So we often see him with a coat of one color, trousers of another and a hat of another, with no gloves at all and his tie missing.

Often Absent-Minded

We have always said people were "absent-minded" when their minds were absent from what they were doing. This often applies to the Brainy for he is capable of greater concentration than other types;

also he is so frequently compelled to do things in which he has no interest that his mind naturally wanders to the things he cares about.

Some Brainy professors sometimes appeared before his classes in bedroom slippers or mismatched socks. A Flushed would not be likely to let his own brother catch him in his!

Writes Better than He Talks

The poor talker sometimes surprises us by being a good writer. Such a one is usually of the Brainy type. He likes to think out every phase of a thing and put it into just the right words before giving it to the world. So, many a Brainy man who does little talking outside his intimate circle does a good deal of surreptitious writing. It may be only the keeping of a diary, jotting down memorandum or writing long letters to his friends, but he will write something. Some of the world's greatest ideas have come to light first in the forgotten manuscripts of people of this type who died without showing their writings to anyone. Evidently they did not consider them of sufficient importance or did not care as much about publishing them as about putting them down.

A Die-hard Reader

Visiting offices or homes of the Brainy, you will likely find stacks of books everywhere.

Interested in Everything

"I never saw a book without wanting to read it," said a Brainy man. This expresses the interest every person of this type has in the printed page. "I never see a library without wishing I had time to go there and stay till I had read everything in it."

Homo sapiens Alphabet

The Book Worm

So it is small wonder that such a one becomes known early in life as a "book worm." As a little child he takes readily to reading and won't take too much else. Because we all learn quickly what we like, he is soon devouring books for older heads. "Why won't he run and play like other children?" wails Mother, and "That boy ought to be made to join the ball team," scolds Father; but "that boy" continues to keep his nose in a book.

He can talk on almost any subject—when he will—and knows pretty well what is going on in the world at an age when other boys are oblivious to everything but sports and girls.

Old for His Years

The "little old man" or "little old woman" of ten is always a Brainy child. The Fleshy are the babies of the race and never entirely grow up no matter how many years they live. But the Brainy is born old. From infancy he shows more maturity than other children.

Little Sense of Time

The extreme Brainy often has a deficient sense of time. He is less conscious of the passage of the hours than any other type. The Muscular and the Bony often have an almost uncanny time-sense, but the extreme Brainy man often lacks it. Forgetting to wind his watch or to consult it for hours is a familiar habit of this type.

A woman living in an apartment across the street from a bakery in Detroit asks her Brainy hubby to go across the street for the loaf of bread because she realizes that they do not have any bread right before dinner. She waits for hours and then has him come back with a book under his arm, no bread and no realization of how long he had been gone.

Inclined to be Unorthodox

Other types tend to follow various religions—according to the individual's upbringing—but the Brainy usually composes a large percentage of the unorthodox.

The Political Reformer

Because all forms of personal combat are distasteful to him the pure Brainy does not go out and fight for reform as often as the Muscular or die for causes as often as the Bony types. But almost every Brainy believes in extreme reforms of one kind or another. He is a comparatively silent but faithful member of clubs, leagues and other kinds of reform organizations. He may never star in them. He seldom cares to. But his wallet is ready when subscriptions are taken, even if he has to go without breakfast for a week to make up for it.

This type is usually sufficiently intelligent to know the world needs reforming and sufficiently conscientious to want to help to do it. He is not bound by traditions or customs as much as other types but does more of his own thinking. Without the foresight and faithfulness of the Brainy very few reforms could have started or have lived to finish.

The World's Pathfinder

Homo sapiens Alphabet

The Brainy therefore leads the world in ideas. The world is managed by the Fleshy men, entertained by the Flushed men, built by the Muscular men, opposed by the Bony men, but is improved in the final analysis by its thinking men.

These thinkers have a difficult time of it. They preach to deaf ears. And often they die in poverty. But at last posterity comes around to their way of thinking, abandons the old ruts and follows the trails they have blazed. Therefore many great thinkers who were unknown while alive became famous after death. More often than not, "Fame is the food of the tomb."

Indifference to Surroundings

A wise man it was who said, "Let me see a man's surroundings and I will tell you what he is." The Brainy does not really live in his house but in his head, and for that reason does not feel as great an urge to decorate, amplify or even furnish the place in which he dwells.

Step into the room of any little-bodied large-headed man and you will be struck by two facts—that he has fewer knickknacks and more journals lying around than the rest of your friends.

In the room of the Fleshy you will find cushions, sofas and food; in that of the Flushed you will find colorful, unusual things; the Muscular will have durable, solid, plain things; the Bony will have fewer of everything but what he does have will be in order.

But the pure Brainy man's furnishings—if he is responsible for them—will be an indifferent array, with no two pieces matching. Furthermore, everything will be piled with newspapers, magazines, books and news clippings.

Homo sapiens Alphabet

The Impersonal

The Brainy is the most impersonal of all types. While the Fleshy tends to measure everything from the standpoint of what it can do for him personally, the Brainy tends to think more impersonally and to be interested in many things outside of his own affairs.

Lacks Aggression

Primitive things of every kind are distasteful to the Brainy. The instincts of digestion, sex, hunting and aggression are but little developed in him. He is therefore a man who likes harmony, avoids coming to confrontation, and goes out of his way to keep the peace. Such a man does not go hunting and seldom owns a gun. He dislikes to kill or to harm any creature.

The Smartest Crook

The Brainy is usually a naturally moral person. But when lacking in conscience, either through bad training or other causes, he occasionally turns to crime for his income. This is because his physical frailty makes it difficult for him to do heavy work, while his mentality enables him to think out ways and means of getting a living without it.

Though the clumsy criminal may belong to any type, the smartest crooks—those who defy detection for years—always have a large element of the Brainy in their makeup.

Look at cartoons that have a character who is a criminal mastermind in it. The criminal mastermind usually is a small scrawny man with a big head commanding his huge muscular cronies.

Big Brains in Little Jobs

There are two kinds of work in the world—head work and hand work; mental and manual. If you can excel in either, life guarantees you a good living. But if you are good at neither you are doomed to dependence. The Brainy man's physical frailty unfits him for the manual and unless he is schooled-or self-educated he becomes the sorriest of all human misfits. He falls between the two and leads a precarious existence working in the lighter indoor positions requiring the least mentality. If you will keep your eyes open you will many times note that the little waiter in the high class restaurant or hotel has a head very large for his body. Such men are much better read, have a far greater appreciation of art and literature and more natural refinement than the porky patrons they serve.

Social Assets

A fine sense of the rights of others and natural modesty and refinement are the chief social assets of this type.

Social Liabilities

Lack of self-expression, too great reserve and too much abstractness in conversation are the things that handicap the Brainy. His small stature and timid air also add to his appearance of insignificance and cause him to be overlooked at social affairs.

Emotional Assets

Sympathy, gentleness and self-sacrifice are other assets of this type.

Emotional Liabilities

Homo sapiens Alphabet

A tendency of nervous excitement and a lack of balance are the chief emotional handicaps of this type.

Business Assets

This type has no traits which can properly be called business assets. He dislikes business, is repelled by its standards and has no place in any of its purely commercial branches.

Business Liabilities

His inability to "keep his feet on the ground," and his tendency to "live in the clouds" and to be generally impractical unfit this type for business life.

His Strong Points

His thinking capacity, progressiveness, unselfishness, and highly civilized instincts are the strong points of this type.

His Weak Points

Impracticality, dreaminess, physical frailty and his tendency to plan without doing are the traits which stand in the way of his success.

How to Deal with this Type Socially

Don't expect him to be a social lion. Don't expect him to mingle with many. Invite him when there are to be a few congenial souls, and if he wanders into the library leave him alone.

How to Deal with this Type in Business

Don't employ this man for heavy manual labor or where there is more physical work than head work. Give him mental positions or none.

Remember, the chief distinguishing marks of the Brainy, in the order of their importance, are the HIGH FOREHEAD and a PROPORTIONATELY LARGE HEAD FOR THE BODY. Any person who has these is largely of the Brainy type no matter what other types may be included in his makeup.

Homo sapiens Alphabet

TO UNDERSTAND COMBINATIONS

Determine which type PREDOMINATES in a subject.

If there is any doubt in your mind about this do these four things:

1st. Note the body build—which one of the five body types does he most resemble?

(In doing this it will aid you if you will note whether flesh, bone or muscle predominates in his bodily structure.)

2nd. Decide which of the five typical faces his face most resembles.

3rd. Decide which of the five typical hands his hands most resemble.

4th. If still undecided, note his voice, gestures and movements and they will leave no doubt in your mind as to which of these types comes first and which second.

Having decided which type predominates and which is second in him, the significance of this combination is made clear to you by the following law:

Law of Combination

The type PREDOMINATING in a person determines WHAT he does throughout his life—the NATURE of his main activities.

The type which comes second in development will determine the WAY he does things—the METHODS he will follow in doing what his predominant type signifies.

The third element, if noticeable, merely "flavors" his personality.

For example, a Brainy-Muscular-Fleshy does MENTAL things predominantly throughout his life, but in a more MUSCULAR way than if he were an extreme Brainy. The Fleshy element, being third down the list, will tend to make him eat and assimilate more food than he otherwise would. This is a good combination because the Mental can dream up idea and the Muscular makes it happen. Many great artists and inventors are this combination.

CONCLUSION:

Now that you understand the 5 different types of human physical traits and their correlated behaviors under general circumstances, internalize them. Practice by observing your friends or family members whom you know their behaviors well. Figure out what their physical type or combination of types they are and their supposedly correlated behaviors and see how accurate you are. You must identify which is the predominant physical type and which is the secondary one to correctly understand them. If you are wrong, find out where you go wrong and correct your mistakes. Once you fine tune your observation skill to be able to identify people's type or combination of types quickly and accurately, you will have the clear and deep understanding of your clients' needs and wants and their preferred method of collaboration. This will definitely help you gain the trust and confidence of your clients who will be your clients for life and refer other clients to you. For example, if you are working with a predominantly muscular type, you must do what you say you will do, do not put on an air of superiority or they will snub you, be straight forward with them, keep things simple and efficient, and do not antagonize them or will lose them forever.

Homo sapiens Alphabet

We know that all dogs belong to the same species; but how many of us actually know the typical behaviors of each breed? How does a St. Bernard behave? How does a Labrador behave? How does a Terrier behave? Dog lovers who put effort into learning about the different behaviors of each breed of dog will undoubtedly be able to differentiate these breeds and behaviors.

So, you too can put an effort into learning how to understand your fellowmen's behaviors based on their physical traits. Reading a book doesn't automatically make you smart. Put what you learn from reading this book into practice will make you smart and earn you as many clients as you can successfully serve without sacrificing the quality of service and give you an edge over other salesmen. Go put your freshly learned skills to work for you.

Good luck.

www.ingramcontent.com/pod-product-compliance
Lightning Source LLC
Chambersburg PA
CBHW051314170526
45166CB00002B/535